LEGAL SERVICES

The
University of
Law

LEGAL SERVICES
FIFTH EDITION

Jacqueline Kempton

This edition published 2025 by
The University of Law
2 Bunhill Row
London EC1Y 8HQ

British Library Cataloguing in Publication Data

A catalogue record for this book is available from the British Library.

ISBN 978 1 80502 258 9

Preface

This book is part of a series of Study Manuals that have been specially designed to support the reader to achieve the SQE1 Assessment Specification in relation to Functioning Legal Knowledge. Each Study Manual aims to provide the reader with a solid knowledge and understanding of fundamental legal principles and rules, including how those principles and rules might be applied in practice.

This Study Manual covers the Solicitors Regulation Authority's syllabus for the SQE1 assessment for Legal Services in a concise and tightly focused manner. The Manual provides a clear statement of relevant legal rules and a well-defined road map through examinable law and practice. The Manual aims to bring the law and practice to life through the use of example scenarios based on realistic client-based problems and allows the reader to test their knowledge and understanding through single best answer questions that have been modelled on the SRA's sample assessment questions.

For those readers who are students at the University of Law, the Study Manual is used alongside other learning resources and the University's assessment bank to best prepare students not only for the SQE1 assessments, but also for a future life in professional legal practice.

We hope that you find the Study Manual supportive of your preparation for SQE1 and we wish you every success.

The legal principles and rules contained within this Manual are stated as at 1 May 2025.

Contents

Table of Cases

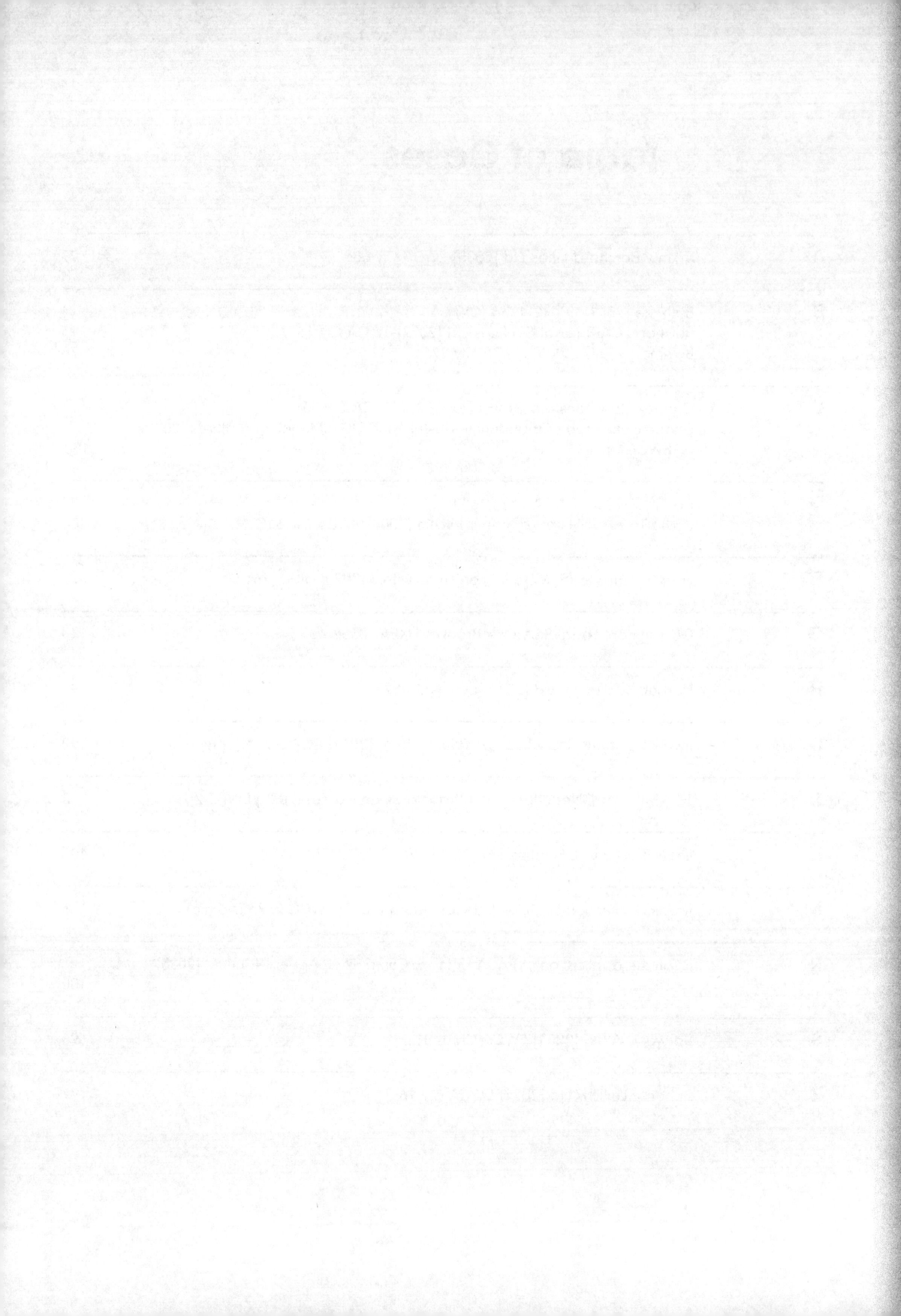

Table of Legislation, Codes and Rules

1

Providers of Legal Services

SQE1 syllabus

This chapter will enable you to achieve the SQE1 Assessment Specification in relation to Functioning Legal Knowledge concerned with Legal Services:

*   The regulatory role of the Solicitors Regulation Authority.
*   Reserved legal activities.
*   Other regulated providers of legal services.

Note that for SQE1, candidates are not usually required to recall specific case names or cite statutory or regulatory authorities. However, in this chapter the following may be referred to in the SQE1 assessments: Legal Services Act 2007. Cases are provided for illustrative purposes only.

Learning outcomes

By the end of this chapter you will be able to apply relevant core legal principles and rules appropriately and effectively, at the level of a competent newly qualified solicitor in practice, to realistic client-based and ethical problems and situations in the following areas:

*   The legal services market.
*   Regulation under the Legal Services Act 2007.
*   Reserved legal activities.
*   Approved regulators.
*   Legal service providers.

1.1 Introduction

The legal services market has gone through successive periods of significant change in recent years. Legal work was once almost exclusively conducted by solicitors and barristers. They continue to occupy the largest part of the sector in England and Wales and their numbers have increased in response to a growing demand for legal services. That demand is a product of a number of factors, including globalisation of the economy, the incorporation/adoption of EU law, increasing affluence and the internet age. However, these factors, together with a political desire to increase competition, have also brought others into the market. Now clients are able to look to an increasing range of providers delivering legal services in both traditional and innovative of ways.

This chapter looks at:

- overview of legal services
- regulated legal activities
- the Legal Services Board
- regulated providers
- regulation outside the Legal Services Act 2007
- unregulated providers

1.2 Overview of legal services

There is no fixed definition of 'legal services'. At its widest, the term embraces all manner of advice, assistance and representation relating to the law. It therefore covers a huge range of activities, from representation before the Supreme Court to the completion of an online court form; from the negotiation of a multimillion-pound contract to writing a will. At the margins it can be difficult to identify a legal service; for example, it is debateable whether the provision of online information falls within its ambit.

Legal services are provided in a variety of ways. The traditional images of a solicitor in an office sitting face to face with a client, or a barrister in wig and gown appearing before a court still hold true. However, conventional law firms are increasingly employing technology, for example to carry out case management, gather information or carry out online triage. There has also been a significant increase in the provision of online services for, for example, document preparation, predictive case outcomes, contract management, and even dispute resolution.

In many instances those who provide services to the public in the UK are subject to regulation. For example, financial services (see **Chapter 4**), transport, utilities and social care all have independent regulators appointed to oversee the provision of those services sector-wide. The role of an independent regulator is essentially to protect the public. Depending on the context, a regulator may set standards for the delivery of the service, set pricing levels, deal with complaints from members of the public and have oversight of the qualification/training of the individuals delivering the service. The underlying justification is that consumers are entitled to expect that services will be delivered to them at a satisfactory standard by those who are properly qualified.

Consumers of legal services have the same expectations; however, legal services are something of a hybrid. The framework for the regulation of legal services is contained in the Legal Services Act 2007. Under the Act a key distinction to be made is between those legal services which fall within the definition of 'reserved legal activities' (see **1.3**) and those which do not. Those services which fall within the definition can only be provided by those who are authorised to do so and who will be subject to regulation as a consequence. Those services which fall outside the definition can be provided by anyone without any legal regulation.

Irrespective of any regulatory requirements, the provision of legal services falls within the framework of the general law. Providers may therefore be subject to overriding legal obligations affecting the way in which they work, for example under the Equality Act 2010 (see **Chapter 3**) and anti-money laundering legislation (see **Chapter 5**).

1.3   Reserved legal activities

In the past the provision of significant aspects of legal work were 'reserved', so that such work could only be carried out by solicitors (and barristers). However, with the opening up of the legal services market over the years this 'monopoly' has been eroded. 'Reserved' legal work still remains, but it is no longer the exclusive preserve of solicitors.

The classification of legal work as 'reserved' is to a large extent historical. However, it is also risk-based. Essentially reserved legal activities comprise those types of legal work where the risk to the public is the greatest.

1.3.1   Definition

There are six types of legal work set out in s 12 Legal Services Act 2007 and defined as 'reserved legal activities':

(a)   The exercise of a right of audience

This means the right to appear before and address a court including the right to call and examine witnesses.

(b)   The conduct of litigation

This means:

- issuing of proceedings before any court in England and Wales;
- the commencing, prosecuting and defending of those proceedings; and
- the performing of any ancillary functions in relation to those proceedings (such as entering appearances to actions).

Media Protection Services Ltd v Crawford [2012] EWHC 2373 (Admin)

The Football Association Premier League brought a private prosecution against the landlord of a public house for infringing its intellectual property rights by screening a football match. The Football Association Premier League employed a company to investigate such infringements. It was one of the directors of the company who laid information before the magistrates' court which led to the issuing of the summons against the landlord. The court found that the laying of the information constituted 'the commencing of the proceedings'. The director had acted unlawfully in carrying out a reserved legal activity whilst unauthorised. The private prosecution itself was therefore held to be unlawful.

A contrasting case is:

JK v MK and E-Negotiation Ltd (trading as amicable) [2020] EWFC 2

A husband and wife used an online divorce facilitator to assist in the drafting of the documents necessary to obtain their divorce and the court order to effect the financial aspects of their separation. The key aspect here was that, in contrast to the case above, all the documents were lodged at court by the parties themselves. The court held that therefore the unregulated company behind the online facilitator had not been engaged in the conduct of litigation.

(c)   Reserved instrument activities

This encompasses preparing and lodging an instrument (formal legal document) dealing with the transfer or charge of land (eg a contract for the sale of land), relating to real or personal estate or an instrument relating to court proceedings. Some types of documents, such as wills and powers of attorney, are excluded.

(d)   Probate activities

This means preparing 'probate papers', ie the documents needed to obtain a grant of probate or a grant of letters of administration or documents to oppose such a grant.

(e)   Notarial activities

This relates to the activities which, prior to the Legal Services Act 2007, were customarily carried on by notaries under the Public Notaries Act 1801. Those activities essentially relate to certifying and authenticating certain documents.

(f)   The administration of oaths

This is the power to administer an oath, for example when a document, such as an affidavit, is required to be sworn.

1.3.2   Authorisation

Under s 13 Legal Services Act 2007 reserved legal activities can only be carried out by those who are authorised or exempt.

A person must be authorised to carry out a particular reserved legal activity by a relevant approved regulator (s 18 Legal Services Act 2007). The Act lists approved regulators for specific reserved legal activities (see **1.5**). An authorised person is subject to the regulatory requirements of their own regulator in respect of all the legal services they provide, including those which fall outside the definition of reserved legal activity.

The Law Society is the approved regulator for solicitors named in the Legal Services Act 2007, but the regulatory function is carried out in practice by the Solicitors Regulation Authority (SRA). The SRA deals with authorisation for all the reserved legal activities except notarial activities.

Section 19 Legal Services Act 2007 lists the circumstances in which a person is exempt in relation to each of the reserved legal activities. For example, in relation to rights of audience a person will be exempt if a court grants that person a right of audience in a particular case (eg a McKenzie friend); in relation to probate activities an exemption allows an employee to act under the supervision of an authorised person. There is also an exemption for some non-commercial organisations such as charities and independent trade unions.

It is a criminal offence for a person to carry on a 'reserved legal activity' if that person is neither authorised nor exempt (s 14 Legal Services Act 2007). The offence is punishable by up to two years' imprisonment. Additionally, in the context of rights of audience and conduct of litigation, carrying out a reserved legal activity whilst not entitled to do so places the individual in contempt of court.

Re Balli [2011] EWHC 1736 (Ch)

In this case, despite having SRA authorisation withdrawn and being struck off by the Solicitors' Disciplinary Tribunal, a solicitor continued to provide legal services and conduct litigation for his clients. In his judgment HH Judge Simon Barker QC said: 'He nevertheless continued to masquerade as a solicitor before the court and in dealings with other legal representatives engaged in ongoing proceedings. In so doing, he deceived the court, counsel he instructed, and opposing representatives, albeit not his own clients. These are extremely serious matters.' The court imposed a six-month prison sentence for contempt of court.

1.4   The Legal Services Board

The Legal Services Board (LSB) is responsible for overseeing the regulation of all lawyers in England and Wales. There are eight separate regulators directly regulating the different types of lawyer on a day-to-day basis.

The LSB was created by the Legal Services Act 2007. The LSB is given various statutory responsibilities including ensuring standards of regulation. A body can only act as a regulator for legal services under the Legal Services Act 2007 if it is approved by the LSB. The LSB therefore oversees and coordinates the regulation of legal services.

In exercising any of its functions the LSB has a duty to promote the regulatory objectives set out in s 1 Legal Services Act 2007:

- protecting and promoting the public interest;
- supporting the constitutional principle of the rule of law;
- improving access to justice;
- protecting and promoting the interests of consumers;
- promoting competition in the provision of services in the legal sector;
- encouraging an independent, strong, diverse, and effective legal profession;
- increasing public understanding of citizens' legal rights and duties;
- promoting and maintaining adherence to the professional principles;
- promoting the prevention and detection of economic crime.

Individual regulators are set the same objectives and the LSB will hold them to account. The LSB monitors the way in which the regulators operate and can make recommendations for improvement, impose penalties for deficiencies or ultimately withdraw approval. The LSB exercises control over the regulators, for example it must give consent to any regulatory changes.

1.5   Regulated providers

In essence regulation is intended to protect the public by ensuring those providing legal services meet professional standards. Regulated individuals must comply with their own regulator's regulatory arrangements on such subjects as education and training requirements, a code of conduct, framework to practice and provision for disciplinary and enforcement action. Firms are primarily responsible for ensuring compliance with regulators, but individuals within those firms are responsible for their own conduct.

A variety of providers of legal services are subject to regulation by regulators approved by the LSB. Each of the approved regulators is linked to a particular profession or specialisation. The need for regulation arises because the provider is carrying out reserved legal activities; however, almost invariably, a provider will additionally be doing work which falls outside the definition. Regulated individuals are subject to regulatory requirements in respect of all the legal services they provide, not just those falling within the definition of reserved legal activities.

1.5.1   Solicitors

As a group, solicitors are the largest providers of legal services. The work of solicitors and the regulatory role of the SRA are considered in detail in **Chapter 2.**

1.5.2 Barristers

The primary role of barristers is as advocates in the criminal and civil courts. They also provide expert legal advice and draft documentation. Traditionally members of the public had to employ a solicitor to instruct a barrister on their behalf. However, in certain circumstances, an individual may now instruct a 'public access barrister' direct.

Most barristers are self-employed and work in sets of chambers sharing premises and administrative facilities. Some barristers are employed by such bodies as the Civil Service, the Crown Prosecution Service, law firms and companies.

The approved regulator for barristers is the Bar Standards Board. It can authorise barristers to provide all types of reserved legal activity, except notarial activities.

1.5.3 Chartered legal executives

The work carried out by chartered legal executives is similar to that carried out by solicitors. They interview clients, draft documents, prepare cases etc and often specialise in a particular area of law. Chartered legal executives cannot work independently so they work within law firms under the supervision of a solicitor (although they can be involved in ownership of a firm).

The approved regulator for chartered legal executives is CILEx Regulation. It can authorise chartered legal executives to provide all types of reserved legal activity, except notarial activities.

1.5.4 Licensed conveyancers

Licensed conveyancers deal with property transactions. The approved regulator for licensed conveyancers is the Council for Licensed Conveyancers. It can authorise licensed conveyancers to conduct reserved instrument activities, probate activities and the administration of oaths.

1.5.5 Patent attorneys

Patent attorneys are specialists in patents and intellectual property. The approved regulator for patent attorneys is the Intellectual Property Regulation Board. It can authorise patent attorneys to conduct all reserved legal activity except probate and notarial activities.

1.5.6 Trade mark attorneys

Trade mark attorneys are specialists in trade mark law and practice. The approved regulator for trade mark attorneys is the Intellectual Property Regulation Board. It can authorise trade mark attorneys to conduct all reserved legal activity except probate and notarial activities.

1.5.7 Costs lawyers

Costs lawyers are specialists in legal fees and costs. They may, for example, prepare bills and costs estimates, appear before the court when costs are assessed and attend case management conferences. The approved regulator for costs lawyers is the Costs Lawyers Standards Board. It can authorise costs lawyers to exercise rights of audience, conduct litigation and administer oaths.

1.5.8 Notaries

For historical reasons notaries are appointed by the Archbishop of Canterbury. Notaries authenticate and certify signatures and documents, often where there is a foreign element. They commonly deal with powers of attorney, bills of exchange and documents dealing with foreign property and international finance. The approved regulator for notaries is the Master of the Faculties. It can authorise notaries to carry out all reserved legal activities except exercising rights of audience and conducting litigation. The Master of Faculties is the only regulator that can authorise notarial activities.

1.5.9   Chartered accountants

Chartered accountants can be authorised by the Institute of Chartered Accountants in England and Wales to carry out probate activities.

1.5.10   Regulatory overlap

Given the way in which firms or bodies are set up there is a degree of overlap between the regulators. This means that, whilst an individual is regulated by their own approved regulator, the firm for which they work is regulated by another. For example, a barrister may work in a firm of solicitors; the barrister would be regulated by the Bar Standards Board, whilst the firm would be authorised by the SRA.

1.6   Regulation outside the Legal Services Act 2007

Some providers carry out work which falls outside the Legal Services Act 2007 but they are nevertheless subject to specific statutory legal regulation. The main examples are:

Claims management companies – regulated by the Financial Conduct Authority.

Immigration advisers – regulated by the Office of the Immigration Services Commissioner.

Insolvency practitioners – regulated by the Insolvency Practitioners Association.

1.7   Unregulated providers

Not all legal services are subject to regulation. Unregulated legal services providers conduct work outside the areas of reserved legal activities under the Legal Services Act 2007. Typical examples are will writing, family law advice and employment law advice. The unregulated sector of the legal services market is thought to be substantial. Depending on the definition of 'legal services' some estimates place the unregulated sector at least on a par with the regulated sector.

A whole variety of providers are delivering legal services in the unregulated sector. Whilst, no doubt, some of these are intent on bypassing regulation in order to provide a low-quality service and maximise profits, this is by no means the case across the sector. The vast majority of providers operate in a completely ethical manner. Many individuals providing legal services in the unregulated sector have legal qualifications in that they are former or non-practising lawyers or law graduates. Some groups of providers submit to voluntary self-regulation, for example will-writers and mediators. Self-regulation often mimics statutory regulation in terms of having a code of conduct, complaints process and even indemnity insurance (see **Chapter 2**).

Summary

- The Legal Services Board oversees and coordinates the regulation of legal services according to the regulatory objectives set out in the Legal Services Act 2007.
- Reserved legal activities are:
  - the exercise of a right of audience
  - the conduct of litigation
  - reserved instrument activities
  - probate activities

- ◦ notarial activities
- ◦ the administration of estates

- Reserved legal activities can only be carried out by those authorised by an approved regulator.
- The approved regulators are:

  - ◦ Solicitors Regulation Authority
  - ◦ Bar Standards Board
  - ◦ CILEx Regulation
  - ◦ Council for Licensed Conveyancers
  - ◦ Intellectual Property Regulation Board
  - ◦ Costs Lawyers Standards Board
  - ◦ Master of Faculties

Sample questions

Question 1

Three friends decide to set up a firm offering conveyancing services to members of the public. None of the friends are solicitors.

Which of the following best describes the position regarding the regulatory requirements which will apply to the proposed firm?

A   The firm must be authorised by the SRA.

B   There is no need for the firm to be authorised.

C   The firm must be authorised by the Legal Services Board.

D   The firm must be authorised by an approved regulator.

E   Authorisation for the firm is dealt with outside the Legal Services Act 2007.

Answer

Option D is correct. As the firm will be offering conveyancing services it will be carrying out reserved instrument activities – one of the reserved legal activities. The firm must therefore be authorised (option B is wrong) within the regulatory framework set down by the Legal Services Act 2007 (option E therefore is wrong). Authorisation can be given by any of the approved regulators (here probably the Council of Licensed Conveyancers) and is not restricted to the SRA (option A therefore is not the best answer). Option C is wrong as the Legal Services Board is responsible for the oversight of regulation; it does not authorise firms itself.

Question 2

A solicitor is authorised to provide legal services by the SRA.

Which of the following best describes the effect of authorisation?

A   The solicitor can provide all reserved legal activities.

B   The solicitor will be subject to regulation by the SRA in respect of all the legal services they provide.

C   The solicitor is only subject to regulation by the Legal Services Board in respect of the reserved legal activities they carry out.

D   The solicitor is absolved from the need to comply with any further regulatory requirements.

E   The solicitor is only subject to regulation by the SRA in respect of the reserved legal activities they carry out.

Answer

Option B is correct. An authorised provider is subject to regulation by their own regulator (here the SRA) in respect of all the legal services they provide, not just those falling within the definition of reserved legal activities. The SRA cannot authorise an individual to carry out notarial activities, and so the solicitor cannot carry out all types of reserved legal activity.

2 The Regulatory Role of the Solicitors Regulation Authority

SQE1 syllabus

This chapter will enable you to achieve the SQE1 Assessment Specification in relation to Functioning Legal Knowledge concerned with Legal Services:

- The regulatory role of the Solicitors Regulation Authority.
- Principles and risk-based regulation.
- Professional indemnity insurance.

Note that for SQE1, candidates are not usually required to recall specific case names or cite statutory or regulatory authorities. However, in this chapter the following may appear in the SQE1 assessments: SRA Code of Conduct for Solicitors, RELs and RFLs. Cases are provided for illustrative purposes only.

Learning outcomes

By the end of this chapter you will be able to apply relevant core legal principles and rules appropriately and effectively, at the level of a competent newly qualified solicitor in practice, to realistic client-based and ethical problems and situations in the following areas:

- The role of the SRA.
- The need for authorisation.
- Professional indemnity insurance provision.

2.1 Introduction

The SRA regulates solicitors, the firms in which they work (and the non-lawyers they employ) and registered European and foreign lawyers. This chapter focuses on the SRA's role as an approved regulator under the Legal Services Act 2007 (see **Chapter 1**) in authorising individuals and firms to provide legal services.

This chapter looks at:

- the Solicitors Regulation Authority
- risk-based regulation
- firm-based authorisation
- authorisation of individuals
- solicitors outside authorised firms
- professional indemnity insurance

2.2 The Solicitors Regulation Authority

In the past, regulation of the profession was in the hands of the Law Society. The Law Society was founded in 1825 to raise the reputation of the profession. The Law Society had a dual function, as both the regulator of the profession and the representative body for solicitors in England and Wales. Over time, however, a view took hold that there was an inherent conflict in the same organisation fulfilling both these roles. With the introduction of the Legal Services Act 2007 the roles had to be separated. Consequently, the SRA was established by The Law Society in January 2007 as an independent body to take over the regulation of solicitors from the Law Society itself.

In its own words, the purpose of the SRA is to protect and help the public by making sure solicitors and law firms meet high standards and taking action against solicitors who do not follow the rules. The SRA is governed by a board of 10 members. This board comprises four solicitors and six lay members. The headquarters of the SRA are at The Cube, Birmingham, and there is an office in central London. Its budget is funded from the practising certificate fee (see **2.5.2**).

Regulation is underpinned by the SRA Principles which comprise the fundamental tenets of ethical behaviour that is expected of all those regulated by the SRA (see **Ethics and Professional Conduct** for a detailed discussion of the Principles). The Principles require that those regulated by the SRA act:

1. in a way that upholds the constitutional principle of the rule of law, and the proper administration of justice;

2. in a way that upholds public trust and confidence in the solicitors' profession and in legal services provided by authorised persons;

3. with independence;

4. with honesty;

5. with integrity;

6. in a way that encourages equality, diversity and inclusion;

7. in the best interests of each client.

The SRA's role is wide ranging. For example, it controls training and admission to the profession, sets standards for ethical and professional behaviour (see **Ethics and Professional Conduct**), frames rules for handling of client money (see **Solicitors Accounts**), supervises firms and takes enforcement action where appropriate. The SRA is an approved regulator under the Legal Services Act 2007 and, as such, is empowered to authorise solicitors and firms to carry out 'reserved legal activities' (see **1.3**).

As an approved regulator, the SRA operates under the oversight of the Legal Services Board. In exercising any of its functions, the LSB has a duty to promote the regulatory objectives set out in s 1 Legal Services Act 2007 (see **1.4**). These objectives are passed onto the SRA as an approved regulator. In discharging its regulatory functions, the SRA must, as far as is reasonably practicable, act in a way which is compatible with the objectives.

Although the legislation sets regulatory objectives, it does not stipulate the purpose of legal services regulation. In a policy statement in 2015, the SRA said:

In the SRA's view, the purpose of its regulation is to:

- protect consumers of legal services; and

- support the operation of the rule of law and the proper administration of justice.

Those dual purposes reflect the fact that poor quality legal services have an impact on both the individual and the justice system as a whole.

2.3   Risk-based regulation

The SRA takes a risk-based approach to regulation. This means that in exercising its regulatory functions the SRA assesses the risk to the SRA achieving its regulatory objectives (see **2.2**). The focus is on misconduct most likely to harm the public interest. The SRA is then able to target its resources where the risk is the greatest.

Risk is a combination of the impact of a certain event occurring (the potential harm that could be caused) and the probability that the event will occur (the likelihood of the event occurring). This combination enables the SRA to measure the risk posed in any given situation, set its priorities and select a response.

Risks in the delivery of legal services can take a variety of forms. For example, the risks arising from:

- the way a firm is structured and its viability;

- a firm or individual becoming involved in fraud or dishonesty;

- the people, systems and internal processes of a firm;

- individuals lacking the requisite skills, knowledge or behaviours;

- the way the legal market operates;

- factors, such as economic, political or legal change.

The SRA identifies risk involved in any given situation based on the range of information it holds, receives or can gather about those it regulates. It looks at problems which have actually arisen or factors which pose potential problems for the future. The SRA will then assess the risk involved and target its resources appropriately. For example, the SRA may identify a risk because a firm is the subject of a number of complaints, assess the risk as high because the firm is large and therefore a large number of people could be affected and then conclude that it needs to devote resources to work with the firm to ensure that its procedures are improved.

Risk identification covers multiple levels: individual solicitors, firms and profession-wide. So, risk will be assessed when the SRA is deciding what, if any, limitations need to be placed on an individual's practising certificate, whether a firm should be closed down and whether changes need to be made to the Codes of Conduct. The SRA can use a variety of measures to proportionately address the issues or reduce the risk, eg set standards, impose fines, issue warning notices or raise consumer awareness.

The SRA aims to be proactive and address issues before they become problems. Each year the SRA publishes its Risk Outlook in which it sets out its view of the most significant risks affecting the profession.

The SRA also expects firms to engage in their own risk management. Paragraph 2.5 of the SRA Code of Conduct for Firms requires a firm to identify, monitor and manage all material risks to its business.

2.4 Firm-based authorisation

As an approved regulator the SRA is able to authorise firms as well as individuals.

2.4.1 Eligible businesses

Under the SRA Authorisation of Firms Rules only certain types of businesses are eligible for authorisation. These are as follows:

2.4.1.1 Recognised sole practice

A sole practitioner is a solicitor who chooses to practise alone. The solicitor will almost certainly employ administration staff, such as secretaries, etc and may also employ other solicitors or paralegals. However, the solicitor will own, and therefore be responsible for, the firm in its entirety.

Whilst sole practitioners used to be very common, there is a general trend for solicitors to practise in larger organisations. There are a number of reasons for this. One prominent reason is cost. In recent times, a solicitor's practice has become more reliant on information technology. Solicitors' firms use such equipment for researching legal issues, for running sophisticated accounts computer packages, and for the day-to-day management of clients' files. Both the hardware and software required to perform these operations are expensive. Accordingly, it is easier to share this cost out amongst a number of partners, rather than for one person to cover the entire cost.

Another reason is practicality. When a partner, or other fee earner, in a law firm goes on holiday, their clients' matters may temporarily be taken over by another solicitor within the firm. The sole practitioner may not have this option. Accordingly, the sole practitioner may have to arrange for a locum solicitor to supervise their absence from the office.

There is also a growing trend for solicitors to specialise in one particular area of law, for example family law or insolvency. Unless the sole practitioner is running a niche practice, this option is not open to them.

Sole practitioners are authorised under the same authorisation rules as other types of firm. Accordingly, their organisation is authorised by the SRA as a 'recognised sole practice' rather than recognising the individual as a sole practitioner.

2.4.1.2   Recognised body

A recognised body is one which is recognised by the SRA under s 9 Access to Justice Act 1985. Under the SRA Authorisation of Firms Rules, a firm is eligible to apply for authorisation as a recognised body where all of the managers and interest holders are legally qualified and, usually, the firm intends to provide legal services.

A recognised body may take the following forms:

(a)   Partnerships

Many solicitors' firms operate as partnerships. The firm is owned and run by the partners, who then employ other solicitors and administration staff to work for them. As the partners own the firm, they are entitled to share the profits generated by the firm between them.

Some large firms have two types of partners – 'equity' partners and 'salaried' partners. A salaried partner is the first step on the partnership ladder. A salaried partner may not be entitled to share in the profits of the firm, but they will receive a salary from the firm in excess of that paid to other non-partner fee earners. After a number of years, a salaried partner may be promoted to an equity partner, whereupon they will be entitled to share in the profits of the firm.

(b)   Limited liability partnerships

A limited liability partnership (LLP) is an incorporated partnership. Instead of partners, LLPs have members. The members will share in the profits of the LLP. Many of the larger law firms have adopted this business structure in recent years.

(c)   Companies

A solicitors' practice may be incorporated as a company registered under the Companies Act 2006. The company will have directors and shareholders like any other company.

2.4.1.3   Licensed bodies

The concept of alternative business structures (ABSs) was introduced by the Legal Services Act 2007. Despite the name, ABSs operate in much the same way as conventional law firms, although they may be offering legal services alongside non-legal services. The key difference is that the ownership, control or management of an ABS is not wholly in the hands of individuals who are legally qualified.

For a body to be eligible to apply for authorisation as a licensed body, there must be at least one manager who is authorised by the SRA (eg a solicitor) or another approved regulator (eg the Council of Licensed Conveyancers (see **1.5.4**)). It also has to be a 'licensable body'. A body ('B') will be a 'licensable body' if a non-authorised person (ie someone not authorised by the SRA or another approved regulator):

(a)   is a manager of B; or

(b)   is an interest holder of B (eg a person who holds shares in it or is entitled to exercise any voting rights).

Alternatively (or in addition to the above), a body ('B') will be a licensable body if:

(a)   another body ('A') is a manager of B, or is an interest holder of B; and

(b)   non-authorised persons are entitled to exercise, or control the exercise of, at least 10% of the voting rights in A.

2.4.2 Effect of authorisation

Once authorised (and unless the SRA specifies otherwise) a recognised body is entitled to carry on all reserved legal activities (except notarial activities). This term is defined in s 12 of the Legal Services Act 2007 and includes conducting court proceedings, the preparation/lodging of documents relating to the transfer or charging of land and the preparation of probate documents (see **1.3**). Authorisation also enables the firm to carry out immigration work.

The business of a recognised body is limited to:

(a) professional services of the sort provided by individuals practising as solicitors and/or lawyers of other jurisdictions; and

(b) other professional services set out in annex 2 of the Rules, for example alternative dispute resolution, estate agency and financial services.

It must at all times have an individual who is designated as its Compliance Officer for Legal Practice (COLP), and one who is designated as its Compliance Officer for Finance and Administration (COFA) and whom the SRA has approved.

Once authorised, a licensed body is entitled to carry out the same range of activities as a recognised body in accordance with the terms of the licence granted by the SRA. As with recognised bodies, it must at all times have individuals designated as compliance officers, but for licensed bodies these are termed a Head of Finance and Administration (HOFA) and a Head of Legal Practice (HOLP).

2.4.3 The authorisation process

Firms that wish to carry out reserved legal activities (or immigration work) must make an application to the SRA for authorisation.

On receipt of an application the SRA will check that the basic eligibility requirements are met and then carry out an investigation into the firm. The purpose of the investigation is for the SRA to satisfy itself that the firm is suitable to carry out reserved legal activities. In accordance with its risk-based approach to regulation, the precise form that the SRA investigation will take depends on an assessment of the risks involved. In simple terms, where, for example, a firm has weaknesses in its processes or is managed by individuals who have a poor professional conduct history the SRA will devote more of its resources in subjecting the firm to a more rigorous process.

In its Guidance for firms on authorisation, the SRA sets out the key outcomes it is intending to achieve through the authorisation process:

* clients and the general public remain confident that legal services provided by regulated firms will be delivered to the required standard;

* firms will be managed in such a way, and with appropriate systems and controls in place to promote public confidence in legal services;

* those who own and manage law firms have the competence, character and willingness to achieve the right outcomes for clients and third parties;

* only those individuals and firms who/that meet the SRA's criteria for authorisation or approval (including the requirements to be suitable and capable of providing legal services to the required standard) are authorised or approved.

Following its investigation the SRA may grant blanket authorisation, authorise the provision of selected legal services or refuse the application.

Some firms which are not required to be authorised (because of the type of legal services they offer) may nevertheless apply for authorisation with the aim of giving reassurance to its clients.

2.5 Authorisation of individuals

The authorisation of individuals is governed by the SRA Authorisation of Individuals Regulations. In this context authorisation involves admission as a solicitor and obtaining a practising certificate.

These are the same requirements which must be satisfied for an individual to be able to act as a solicitor. Section 1 Solicitors Act 1974 states:

> No person shall be qualified to act as a solicitor unless—
>
> (a) he has been admitted as a solicitor, and
>
> (b) his name is on the roll, and
>
> (c) he has in force a certificate issued by the Society ... authorising him to practise as a solicitor (in this Act referred to as a 'practising certificate').

Any person who does not comply with this section will fall within the definition of an 'unqualified person' (Solicitors Act 1974, s 87) and so cannot practise as a solicitor. Any person who practises as a solicitor without having a practising certificate will commit a criminal offence.

Consequently, anyone who is practising as a solicitor is, by definition, subject to the regulation of the SRA.

2.5.1 Admission

Admission simply means that an individual is accepted into the profession and their name is placed on the list, or roll, of solicitors kept by the SRA. An individual will be admitted to the roll of solicitors if they have attained the required qualifications, undertaken the required training (neither are considered further here) and the SRA is satisfied as to their character and suitability to be a solicitor.

The SRA Assessment of Character and Suitability Rules set out the factors which the SRA will take into account in deciding whether an individual is suitable for admission. The Rules apply to all individuals applying for admission to the roll of solicitors (including those applying to the SRA for an early assessment of their character and suitability). The Rules also apply to those applying to become an authorised role holder in a firm (eg a Compliance Officer for Legal Practice (COLP)) and former solicitors seeking restoration to the roll.

According to Part 1 of the Rules, when considering an individual's character and suitability under the Rules, the SRA will take into account the overriding need to protect the public and the public interest and maintain public trust and confidence in the solicitors' profession and in legal services provided by 'authorised persons'. In doing so, it will take into account the nature of the applicant's role and their individual circumstances on a case-by-case basis.

Part 2 of the Rules sets out the conduct and other behaviour that the SRA will consider when assessing an individual's character and suitability, which fall into two main heads: criminal conduct and other conduct or behaviour. There is a non-exhaustive list in Part 3 of the Rules which sets out the types of aggravating and mitigating factors that the SRA will take into account under either of these heads.

If an applicant has been involved in criminal conduct, the action taken by the SRA will depend upon the type of conduct involved. These are dealt with in the following categories:

- Most serious

    A finding in this category is likely to result in the application being refused. These include where an applicant has been convicted by a court of a criminal offence resulting in a custodial or suspended sentence, involving dishonesty, perjury, fraud and/or bribery, of a violent or sexual nature, associated with obstructing the course of justice, associated with terrorism or which demonstrated behaviour showing signs of discrimination towards others. Also included are cases where a caution has been accepted from the police for an offence involving dishonesty, violence or discrimination or a sexual offence or the applicant has been included on the Violent and Sex Offender register.

- Serious

  A finding in this category may result in the application being refused. These include where a caution has been accepted for, or the individual has been convicted of, a criminal offence not falling within the 'most serious' category and where an individual is subject to a conditional discharge or bind over by a court.

The Rules set out a non-exhaustive list of examples of the other types of conduct and behaviour that the SRA will take into account. These include where:

- the applicant has behaved in a way which is dishonest, violent, threatening or harassing or where there is evidence of discrimination towards others;

- the applicant has committed and/or has been adjudged by an education establishment to have committed a deliberate assessment offence, which amounts to plagiarism or cheating, in order to gain an advantage for himself or others;

- there is evidence that the applicant has deliberately sought to avoid responsibility for their debts, dishonestly managed their finances, been declared bankrupt or cannot satisfactorily manage their finances;

- the applicant has been made the subject of serious disciplinary or regulatory findings or sanctions.

On making an application for admission, an individual must disclose all matters, wherever they have taken place (including overseas), which are relevant to the assessment of character and suitability and provide any further information requested by the SRA by the date specified. Failing to disclose any material information relating to the application will be taken into account by the SRA when making its determination. It is important to note that there is an ongoing obligation on those covered by the Rules to tell the SRA promptly about anything that raises a question about their character and suitability, or any change to information previously disclosed to the SRA.

2.5.2 Practising certificates

An admitted solicitor is eligible to apply to the SRA for a practising certificate if their name is on the roll, they have sufficient knowledge of written and spoken English or Welsh and they are not suspended from practice as a solicitor.

Subject to limited exceptions, the certificate then entitles a solicitor to carry on all 'reserved legal activities' (except notarial activities). In respect of rights of audience, however, although solicitors have rights of audience in all courts, a solicitor cannot exercise those rights in the higher courts (Crown Court, High Court, Court of Appeal and Supreme Court) until they have successfully completed, as appropriate, the Higher Courts (Civil Advocacy) Qualification or the Higher Courts (Criminal Advocacy) Qualification.

Although the practising certificate is personal to the individual, subject to some limited exceptions (see **2.6**), the reserved legal activities must be provided through an authorised body.

The need for reserved legal activities to be provided through an authorised body will be an important consideration for, say, a solicitor who works within a mainstream authorised firm and who wishes to additionally undertake pro bono work. Such work might be conducted through the firm (eg under a programme set up by the firm) in which case there is no issue. However, if not, the solicitor cannot rely on their practising certificate alone and will need to ensure that they fall within and satisfy the requirements of an exception (see **2.6**).

Those who are required to hold a practising certificate must apply to the SRA each year to have their certificates renewed. All practising certificates become due for renewal on 31 October each year. A fee is payable on renewal of the certificate.

A solicitor is obliged to inform the SRA promptly of any material changes to relevant information about themselves or their practice, including any change to information recorded on the roll if the solicitor is subject to any criminal charge, conviction or caution, or if a relevant insolvency event occurs in relation to them (for example, bankruptcy) (Paragraph 7.6 of the SRA Code of Conduct for Solicitors, RELs and RFLs,).

The SRA has a certain level of discretion regarding the issue of practising certificates. If the SRA considers it to be in the public interest to do so, it must refuse an application for a practising certificate or, at any time, it may impose conditions on an existing certificate as it thinks fit. The SRA may impose such conditions if it is satisfied that the solicitor:

(a) is unsuitable to undertake certain activities or engage in certain business or practising arrangements;

(b) is putting, or is likely to put, at risk the interest of clients, third parties or the public;

(c) will not comply with, or requires monitoring of compliance with, the SRA's regulatory arrangements; or

(d) should take specified steps conducive to the regulatory objectives.

The conditions imposed may specify certain requirements to be met or steps to be taken, restrict the carrying on of certain activities, the holding of certain roles or prohibit the taking of specified steps without the SRA's approval.

A decision by the SRA to refuse an application for a practising certificate or to impose conditions on one can be made the subject of an application for a review by the SRA or appealed to the High Court.

2.6   Solicitors working outside authorised firms

2.6.1   Freelance solicitors

A freelance solicitor is one who works on their own. Ordinarily such a solicitor would have to be authorised as a recognised sole practice (see **2.4.1.1**). In some circumstances, however, such authorisation is not required. Under the SRA Authorisation of Individuals Regulations, a freelance solicitor is not required to be authorised as a recognised sole practice if:

(a) their practice consists entirely of carrying on activities which are not 'reserved legal activities'; or

(b) any reserved legal activities are provided through an authorised body; or

(c) certain requirements are met. For example, the solicitor must have practised as a solicitor for a minimum of three years since admission, be self-employed and practise in their own name, take out indemnity insurance in respect of all the services they provide, does not employ anyone in connection with those services and only holds limited categories of client money.

Even when authorisation is not required, a freelance solicitor (other than one providing pro bono services) must notify the SRA of their intention to practise in that capacity. The SRA will place the solicitor's details on a public register.

2.6.2   In-house solicitors

An in-house solicitor is employed by, say, a company or a local authority to provide that employer with legal advice etc. An in-house solicitor is able to deliver reserved legal activities to their employer, but not to the general public.

2.6.3   Non-commercial organisations

'Non-commercial organisation' is defined in s 23(2) Legal Services Act 2007 and includes not-for-profit bodies, charities, community interest groups and independent trade unions. Such organisations are generally exempt from the need to be authorised (see **1.3.2**). Solicitors working directly within non-commercial organisations are allowed, on behalf of the organisation, to provide reserved legal activities to the public.

When providing services to the public these solicitors will be covered by the wider insurance arrangements that organisation has in place. The SRA does not specify a level of cover but does require that the solicitor is covered by professional indemnity insurance that is 'adequate and appropriate' for the work they are carrying out (see **2.7**).

2.6.4 Other organisations

A solicitor is able to work for a commercial unregulated organisation providing legal services to the public. However, such a solicitor cannot carry out reserved legal activities.

2.7 Professional indemnity insurance

2.7.1 The nature of professional indemnity insurance

Professional indemnity insurance is a necessary requirement for many professions, including solicitors. Professional indemnity insurance caters for the possibility that the insured may be guilty of a breach of professional duty which gives rise to financial loss or damage to a third party. In such circumstances the effect of the insurance policy is that the insurer will indemnify the insured in respect of the loss or damage.

For solicitors, professional indemnity insurance covers civil claims made against a solicitor in the course of their practice. Such claims usually arise as a result of negligence on the part of the solicitor. In simple terms, if a solicitor has been negligent in the conduct of a client's case the insurer will pay the amount necessary to compensate the client for the loss suffered. The insurance does not absolve the solicitor from liability; it merely provides a fund from which such liability can be met. As with any insurance policy, if for any reason the insurer does not accept the claim or the amount of insurance cover is insufficient, the solicitor is liable for the shortfall. In addition, indemnity insurance policies usually provide cover for the legal costs of the solicitor defending the claim and, if the defence is unsuccessful, possibly the client's legal costs as well.

Indemnity insurance policies are usually written on an annual basis and they therefore need to be renewed each year. The cover provided is normally in respect of claims made during the year, rather than events occurring during the year. A firm therefore needs to be forward thinking. It will need to have insurance in place in future years to cover claims based on negligent acts occurring today.

Claims against solicitors have the potential to run into millions of pounds. From the firm's perspective, having insurance in place therefore provides a degree of certainty and financial security. However, the central purpose of professional indemnity insurance is to protect the public by ensuring that they are not left without compensation. Clients can be secure in the knowledge that, if something does go wrong, there is sufficient money in place to meet any claim. Professional indemnity insurance therefore helps to maintain confidence in the profession.

2.7.2 SRA Indemnity Insurance Rules

The SRA Indemnity Insurance Rules ('the Rules') apply to firms authorised by the SRA. All SRA authorised firms must take out and maintain professional indemnity insurance that is appropriate for its practice and meets the specific requirements set out in the Rules (qualifying insurance). Individual assistant solicitors, trainees and others employed by a solicitors' practice will be covered by the insurance taken out by the firm.

Under the Rules the insurance must be taken out with one or more participating insurers. These are insurers who are regulated by the Financial Conduct Authority and have an agreement with the SRA to provide insurance on particular terms.

The Rules set out the minimum terms and conditions for the insurance policy. These include a minimum figure for the sum insured. For recognised and licensed bodies (see **2.4.1**) the sum insured for any one claim (exclusive of defence costs) must be at least £3 million and at least £2 million in all other cases. The firm must not exclude or attempt to exclude liability below this minimum level of cover.

A firm must have qualifying insurance in place at all times. This means that the insurance cover must be continuous. The Rules require a firm to put a new policy in place as the current policy comes to an end. If for some reason a firm cannot effect qualifying insurance at the end of the policy period, the minimum terms and conditions will extend the cover for a maximum of 90 days. The firm must inform the SRA that it has entered this extended policy period. The firm can use this time to try to find insurance cover. After 30 days, if no cover can be found, the firm must notify the SRA and cannot take on new work. If, at the end of 90 days, insurance cover still cannot be secured the firm must cease practising.

The SRA can require a firm to produce evidence so that the SRA can be satisfied that the firm is complying with the Rules.

2.7.3 'Adequate and appropriate insurance'

The SRA requires solicitors to take out and maintain professional indemnity insurance that provides adequate and appropriate cover in respect of services they provide. This requirement applies to:

- SRA authorised firms (Rule 3.1 SRA Indemnity Insurance Rules). The Rules include minimum requirements for insurance cover (see above). However, the additional need for insurance cover to be adequate and appropriate may require a firm to go beyond that minimum. The minimum may not be adequate and appropriate in all cases and so a firm may need to take out 'top-up' cover.

- Freelance solicitors (see **2.6.1**) providing reserved legal services to the public (SRA Authorisation of Individuals Regulations).

- Solicitors in non-commercial organisations (see **2.6.3**) providing reserved legal services to the public (Paragraph 5.6 of the SRA Code of Conduct for Solicitors, RELs and RFLs). Here the non-commercial body will arrange the policy, so the duty placed on the solicitor is to ensure that it does so.

What constitutes adequate and appropriate insurance will vary. It is for each firm or solicitor to determine what is needed based on their individual circumstances. This will require a firm to make an assessment based on such factors as the number and type of clients, its history of claims and an estimate of the level of claims that could be made. The assessment must be kept under review because the needs may vary as the firm develops.

An important point to note is that for freelance solicitors and solicitors in a non-commercial body, the obligation to have adequate and appropriate insurance only arises if they provide reserved legal services to the public. However, the need for insurance to be adequate and appropriate applies to all the services that the solicitor provides.

SRA authorised firms cannot exclude or limit their liability to clients below the minimum level under the SRA's minimum terms and conditions (see above). This restriction does not apply to freelance solicitors or solicitors working for non-commercial bodies. There is no restriction on authorised firms capping their liability above the minimum level. If a cap is set, regard must be had to a solicitor's professional conduct obligations. For example, a solicitor must act in the client's best interests (SRA Principle 7) and must not abuse their position by taking unfair advantage of clients (Paragraph 1.2 SRA Code of Conduct for Solicitors, RELs and RFLs).

2.7.4 Client information

Solicitors must be open with their clients about their professional indemnity insurance provision. There are some specific requirements. For example, under the Provision of Services Regulations 2009 (SI 2009/2999) it is necessary to make available to clients information about the firm's compulsory layer of professional indemnity insurance, including details of the insurer and the territorial coverage of its insurance. Under the SRA Transparency Rules freelance solicitors providing reserved legal services to the public must inform their clients that they are not required to meet the SRA's minimum terms and conditions.

However, solicitors are under wider duties to provide clients with information. The firm's indemnity insurance position may be a factor influencing a client's decision with regard to the provision of legal services. For example, a client may be unwilling to instruct a firm in respect of a £10 million claim if the amount of cover under the firm's policy is only £5 million. Solicitors are under a duty to give clients information in a way they can understand and ensure they are in a position to make informed decisions about the services they need, how their matter will be handled and the options available to them (Paragraph 8.6 SRA Code of Conduct for Solicitors, RELs and RFLs. This is also applicable to firms under Paragraph 7.1 SRA Code of Conduct for Firms).

Summary

- The SRA is the approved regulator for solicitors, the firms in which they work (and their non-lawyer employees), Registered European Lawyers and Registered Foreign Lawyers.

- The SRA adopts a risk-based approach to regulation.

- A firm must be authorised by the SRA to carry out reserved legal activities.

- The SRA can authorise recognised sole practices, recognised bodies and licensed bodies.

- The suitability of an individual to be admitted as a solicitor is governed by the SRA Assessment of Character and Suitability Rules.

- Solicitors holding a practising certificate are authorised to carry out reserved legal activities.

- All firms authorised by the SRA must take out and maintain professional indemnity insurance.

- Indemnity insurance cover must meet minimum requirements and be adequate and appropriate.

- Firms must be open with clients about their professional indemnity insurance provision.

Sample questions

Question 1

Having completed all the necessary training requirements a man wishes to apply for admission to the roll of solicitors.

At the end of their final year at university the man was drinking with some fellow students in a local bar. A fight broke out in which the barman was punched in the face and sustained a black eye. The fight was broken up by the other bar staff. The bar owner put the fight down to student 'high spirits' and decided not to call the police; instead they reported the incident to the university authorities. The university carried out an investigation. At first the man denied being in the bar, but CCTV footage showed that it was the man who had punched the barman. The man was formally disciplined by the university. The incident was completely out of character. The man has not been involved in anything similar before or since.

Should the man tell the SRA about the disciplinary proceedings?

A   No, because the man was not convicted of a criminal offence.

B   No, because the incident took place too long ago to be of relevance in assessing the man's character and suitability.

C   No, because the fact that it was an isolated incident demonstrates that the man is of good character.

D   Yes, because there is a risk that the university will inform the SRA.

E   Yes, because the incident is relevant to the assessment of the man's character and suitability.

Answer

Option E is the best answer. The incident and the disciplinary proceedings are relevant in assessing an application irrespective of when they took place (so Option B is not correct). Option A is not correct because the SRA looks at all types of behaviour, not just criminal or recent behaviour. Rule 4.1 sets out examples of 'other conduct and behaviour' including violence, dishonesty and being subject to disciplinary proceedings by a regulatory body. The man's behaviour was violent (punching the barman) and dishonest (lying to the university authorities) and they were disciplined by the university. The fact that the incident has not been repeated will be taken into account by the SRA, but it is not a justification for withholding the information (so, Option C is not correct). Option D is not the best answer because, whilst there is a risk that the university will inform the SRA, this should not be the reason for disclosure – the man is under an obligation to be open and honest.

Question 2

A solicitor decides to set up in business as a sole practitioner carrying out niche private client work for high net worth individuals. The solicitor anticipates that they will regularly be dealing with estates in excess of £20 million. The solicitor will be authorised by the SRA as a recognised sole practice.

Which of the following best describes how the requirements in respect of professional indemnity insurance applies to the solicitor?

A   The solicitor can limit their liability at below £2 million.

B   The cover must be for at least £3 million.

C   The cover will need to be in excess of the minimum terms and conditions set under the SRA Indemnity Insurance Rules.

D   Having taken out professional indemnity insurance the solicitor will be absolved from liability for negligence.

E   The solicitor is not required to meet the minimum terms and conditions set under the SRA Indemnity Insurance Rules.

Answer

Option C is correct. As a recognised sole practice the cover required under the minimum terms and conditions is £2 million. The ability to limit liability below this sum only applies to freelance solicitors. The solicitor is required to take out 'adequate and appropriate insurance'. Given the size of the estates that the solicitor will be dealing with, the cover will need to be in excess of the minimum. Indemnity insurance does not absolve a solicitor from liability for negligence.

Question 3

Having completed all the necessary training requirements, a prospective solicitor has been offered a position as an assistant solicitor in the Family Department of a large firm of solicitors authorised by the SRA. In order to take up the offer, the prospective solicitor will be applying for admission to the roll of solicitors. There is no reason to think that the application will be refused.

Is it necessary for the prospective solicitor to obtain a practising certificate in order to take up the position?

A   Yes, because having a practising certificate is a mandatory prerequisite for being admitted to the roll of solicitors.

B   Yes, because otherwise in taking up the position the prospective solicitor will be committing a criminal offence.

C   Yes, because the firm is authorised by the SRA.

D   No, because given the nature of the job the prospective solicitor will not be carrying out reserved legal activities.

E   No, because the prospective solicitor will not be a partner in the firm.

Answer

Option B is the best answer. The job is that of a solicitor. Section 1 Solicitors Act 1974, inter alia, requires anyone acting as a solicitor to have a practising certificate. Practising as a solicitor without satisfying the requirements of s 1 is a criminal offence. The requirement is not dependent on the firm being SRA authorised (option C is wrong). The requirement applies irrespective of whether the solicitor will be carrying out reserved legal activities (option D is wrong). The requirement applies to employed solicitors as well as partners (option E is wrong). Finally, option A is wrong as it is possible to be on the roll without having a practising certificate.

3 Equality Act 2010

SQE1 syllabus

This chapter will enable you to achieve the SQE1 Assessment Specification in relation to Functioning Legal Knowledge concerned with Legal Services:

* The regulatory role of the Solicitors Regulation Authority.
* Overriding legal obligations.
* The Equality Act 2010.

Note that for SQE1, candidates are not usually required to recall specific case names or cite statutory or regulatory authorities. However, in this chapter the following may be referred to in the SQE1 assessments: Equality Act 2010. Cases are provided for illustrative purposes only.

Learning outcomes

By the end of this chapter you will be able to apply relevant core legal principles and rules appropriately and effectively, at the level of a competent newly qualified solicitor in practice, to realistic client-based and ethical problems and situations in the following areas:

* The main anti-discrimination provisions of the Equality Act 2010.
* The application of the Equality Act 2010 to solicitors.
* The connection between the Equality Act 2010 and professional conduct.

3.1   Introduction

The Equality Act 2010 ('the Act') is concerned both with protecting the rights of the individual and ensuring fair treatment and equality of opportunity for all. The Act is part of the general law applicable to all. However, solicitors have particular duties under the legislation in their capacities as employers and as providers of legal services.

The duties placed on solicitors under the Act are separate from, but obviously closely linked to, their responsibilities with regard to equality, diversity and inclusion under the SRA Principles and the SRA Codes of Conduct (see **Ethics and Professional Conduct**).

This chapter looks at:

- overview of the Act
- the protected characteristics
- prohibited conduct
- duty to make adjustments
- solicitors as service providers
- solicitors as employers
- barristers
- positive action
- overlap with professional conduct

3.2   Overview of the Act

The philosophy which lies behind equality legislation is that everyone has the right to be treated fairly. Achieving that fairness of treatment requires discrimination to be addressed. The primary focus of the Act is to stop discrimination in its various forms. However, the Act does not create an overall ban on discrimination. Instead it controls unjustifiable discrimination in a limited way by outlawing certain types of discrimination for certain purposes. In addition, the Act imposes some positive duties to take steps to achieve equality.

Under the Act discrimination is addressed using the civil law rather than the criminal law. There are some criminal offences associated with discrimination, but these are largely outside the Act, eg inciting racial hatred and some forms of harassment.

The Act enables those who have been wronged to seek redress. The remedy is an individual action taken by the victim. Employment claims are dealt with in the employment tribunal. Non-employment claims are brought in the county court. Claimants are usually seeking damages, but other remedies such as injunctions and declarations may also be appropriate.

In addition, the Equality and Human Rights Commission (EHRC) has some powers to take action against discriminatory practices. The EHRC is an independent statutory body tasked with encouraging equality and diversity and eliminating unlawful discrimination. The EHRC produces guidance on compliance with the Act as well as codes of practice which are taken into account by the courts/tribunals.

The basic overall shape of the Act is to establish a number of personal characteristics which are the subject of protection under the legislation (the 'protected characteristics'). The Act goes on to define certain types of discriminatory behaviour ('prohibited conduct'). The Act then sets out various contexts (work, education etc) in which it will be unlawful to engage in prohibited conduct in relation to a protected characteristic.

3.3 The protected characteristics

Section 4 Equality Act 2010 lists nine personal characteristics which are protected by the remainder of the Act. The list is wide, but finite. Consequently, discrimination based on some characteristic which falls outside s 4 is not unlawful under the Act (but may give rise to professional conduct issues (see **3.10**)).

There is a basic common approach across all the protected characteristics. However, they are not all dealt with in exactly the same way or subject to the same provisions under the detail of the Act. For example, the provisions aimed at discrimination in the context of disability are quite distinct in that they require positive steps to be taken.

The protected characteristics are:

Race

Race is defined in s 9 to include colour, nationality or ethnic or national origins. This is a very wide definition and indeed it allows for one individual to belong to several different racial groups.

The definition is wide, but it is not without limit. For example, the government has never acted upon the requirement in s 9(5) to amend the Act to make caste an aspect of race, preferring, it would seem, to leave it to the judiciary to explore the ambit of 'race'.

Religion and belief

In contrast to race, religion and belief are not defined other than to say that any religion or philosophical belief and an absence of religion or philosophical belief is covered (s 10). The explanatory notes to the Act go further in relation to 'belief' in saying that it must be genuinely held, be a belief as opposed to a view point, relate to a substantial part of human life, attain a certain level of cogency and be worthy of respect.

Sex

This relates to inequality between men and women. 'Man' is defined as 'a male of any age' and 'woman' as 'a female of any age'. In *For Women Scotland Ltd v Scottish Ministers* [2025] UKSC 16, the Supreme Court ruled that the meaning of the terms 'sex', 'man' and 'woman' is biological.

Sexual orientation

Sexual orientation is defined in s 12 as a sexual orientation towards:

* persons of the same sex

* persons of the opposite sex, or

* persons of the same sex and the opposite sex.

This covers heterosexual people as well as homosexual and bi-sexual people. Orientation is wide enough to cover attraction as well as behaviour.

Age

All ages are covered under the legislation. Section 5 provides that the protected characteristic of age refers to belonging to an 'age group'.

Age is dealt with differently in some respects under the Act. This is to reflect that fact that in some instances a difference in treatment based on age can be justified.

Disability

Disability is defined in s 6. A person has a disability if:

* they have a physical or mental impairment; and

* the impairment has a substantial and long-term adverse effect on their ability to carry out normal day to day activities.

This is supplemented by Schedule 1 which, for example, adds definitions of 'long term' and specifies that certain conditions, such as HIV, are a disability.

The definition is quite narrow and arguably does not reflect the common understanding of the term 'disabled'. The phrase 'substantial and long-term adverse effect' sets a high threshold. It is not unknown for discrimination cases based on disability to fail because the victim cannot bring themselves within s 6.

Gender reassignment

This relates to people who are proposing to undergo, are undergoing or have undergone treatment for the purpose of reassigning the person's sex (s 7). The definition does not require the individual to be under medical supervision in order to be protected under the Act.

Marriage/civil partnerships

This relates to discrimination against people on the basis that they are married or in a civil partnership (s 8). It only covers those who are legally married or in a civil partnership. It does not cover any wider marital status and so it does not protect, for example, cohabitants, single people, divorcees, fiancées etc.

Pregnancy and maternity

Pregnancy/maternity is one of the protected characteristics listed in s 4. However, this protected characteristic is treated quite differently under the Act. Pregnancy/maternity is excluded from some elements of the Act and subject to specific protection when this characteristic is particularly relevant.

3.4 Prohibited conduct

The Act outlaws various types of unequal treatment.

3.4.1 Direct discrimination

The basic definition of direct discrimination is in s 13(1) Equality Act 2010:

> A person (A) discriminates against another (B) if, because of a protected characteristic, A treats B less favourably than A treats or would treat others.

Direct discrimination therefore occurs when a person is treated less favourably than someone else would have been in the same situation and the reason for the difference is one of the protected characteristics. This type of unequal treatment could be termed overt or obvious.

There are three elements to the definition of direct discrimination:

- **Comparator**

  The treatment experienced must be different from that of another real or hypothetical person (the comparator). To establish less favourable treatment the victim must compare the treatment they received to the treatment of another person who does not belong to or is not associated with the claimant's protected characteristic.

  This comparison can be to the treatment of another actual person or, if there is no actual comparator available, to the treatment of a hypothetical comparator. The relevant circumstances of the claimant and the comparator should be the same or not materially different.

- **Less favourable**

  The treatment must be less favourable than that afforded to the comparator. Less favourable treatment is a broad concept. Any disadvantage will be sufficient. There is no need to have suffered tangible or material loss. The test for less favourable treatment is objective, so there is no requirement to show that the perpetrator intended to treat the victim less favourably. Motive may, however, be relevant to the issue of remedies. If the perpetrator has behaved in a malicious or oppressive manner, then aggravated damages can be awarded.

- **Protected characteristic**

    The reason for the less favourable treatment must be a protected characteristic. The protected characteristic must be the cause of the treatment; it need not be the sole or main reason for the treatment, but it must have been an influence. Section 13 is wide enough to cover the situation where the victim is assumed to have a protected characteristic even though that is not in fact the case. For example, if an individual is treated less favourably because they are assumed to belong to a particular racial group based on their name this will amount to discrimination even though the assumption is incorrect.

    There is no general defence of justification of direct discrimination save in relation to age. Where the protected characteristic is age there is no discrimination if the treatment was a proportionate way of achieving a legitimate aim (s 13(2) Equality Act 2010).

    More detailed provisions apply in respect of discrimination on the grounds of pregnancy or maternity (ss 17 and 18 Equality Act 2010).

3.4.2 Indirect discrimination

Direct discrimination is overt or obvious and (save in the context of age) cannot be defended or justified. In contrast, indirect discrimination can be said to be much more subtle. Indirect discrimination occurs where conditions are imposed which apply to everyone, but which have the effect of prejudicing members of a particular group.

The basic definition of indirect discrimination is in s 19 Equality Act 2010:

(1) A person (A) discriminates against another (B) if A applies to B a provision, criterion or practice which is discriminatory in relation to a relevant protected characteristic of B's.

(2) For the purposes of subsection (1), a provision, criterion or practice is discriminatory in relation to a relevant protected characteristic of B's if:

  (a) A applies, or would apply, it to persons with whom B does not share the characteristic,

  (b) it puts, or would put, persons with whom B shares the characteristic at a particular disadvantage when compared with persons with whom B does not share it,

  (c) it puts, or would put, B at that disadvantage, and

  (d) A cannot show it to be a proportionate means of achieving a legitimate aim.

In essence, therefore, indirect discrimination occurs when a policy or practice is put in place which is of universal application, but which has an adverse impact on those who share a protected characteristic.

There is the possibility of justifying the action on the basis that it is a proportionate means of achieving a legitimate aim. This requires a balancing exercise between the degree of discrimination caused and the object or aim to be achieved.

An example of indirect discrimination is an employer requiring an employee to work full time. This requirement could disadvantage women as a group, since women in society as a whole bear a greater part of domestic and childcare responsibilities than men and are more likely to want (or need) to work part time. Unless the employer can objectively justify the need for a full-time worker to do the job, the requirement could be indirectly discriminatory against a woman with childcare responsibilities.

The provisions in the Act relating to indirect discrimination do not apply to pregnancy/ maternity. Discrimination based on pregnancy/maternity will fall under direct discrimination.

3.4.3 Disability discrimination

Although a disabled person may be able to bring a claim for direct or indirect discrimination there is an additional definition for disability discrimination in s 15 Equality Act 2010:

> A person (A) discriminates against a disabled person (B) if A treats B unfavourably because of something arising in consequence of B's disability.

It is discrimination to treat a disabled person less favourably not only because of the individual's disability itself but also because of something arising from, or in consequence of, that disability. In contrast to s 13, there is no requirement in s 15 to compare the treatment received by the disabled with the treatment of others.

It is, however, possible to justify less favourable treatment if it can be shown to be a proportionate means of achieving a legitimate aim. For this type of discrimination to occur, the perpetrator must have known, or reasonably be expected to have known, that the disabled person had a disability.

3.4.4 Victimisation

The basic definition of victimisation is in s 27 Equality Act 2010:

> A person (A) victimises another person (B) if A subjects B to a detriment because
>
> (a) B does a protected act, or
>
> (b) A believes that B has done, or may do, a protected act.

A protected act is any of the following:

- bringing proceedings under the Act;
- giving evidence or information in proceedings brought under the Act;
- doing anything which is related to the provisions of the Act;
- making an allegation that another person has done something in breach of the Act.

The victim does not need to have a protected characteristic in order to receive protection from victimisation under the Act.

The term 'detriment' is not defined under the Act, but it would encompass any act which has the effect of putting the individual at a disadvantage or of making their position worse.

✪ Example

Maya is a legal secretary employed by a firm of solicitors. Maya is bringing a claim against the firm under the Equality Act 2010. Maya's claim is that she was passed over by the firm for promotion on account of her race. Karen is also a legal secretary working for the same firm. Karen agrees to give evidence on Maya's behalf. As a consequence, in the firm's next round of pay reviews Karen is singled out and is not given any increase in her salary. Here the firm's actions would amount to victimisation. Karen would be able to bring her own claim against the firm under the Act.

3.4.5 Harassment

Under s 26 Equality Act 2010 harassment occurs when an individual is subjected to a specific form of unwanted conduct which has the effect of violating the individual's dignity, or creating an intimidating, hostile, degrading, humiliating or offensive environment for the individual.

The unwanted conduct must:

- relate to a protected characteristic (except pregnancy/maternity and marriage/civil partnership);
- be of a sexual nature; or
- be of a sexual nature or related to gender reassignment or sex and result in less favourable treatment because of the individual's rejection of or submission to the conduct.

3.5 Duty to make adjustments

The Equality Act 2010 is for the most part negative in that, after the event, it judges certain behaviour to have been unfair and therefore unlawful. However, in relation to disability, in some circumstances the Act imposes a positive duty to take steps to avoid unfairness occurring in the first place. This is the duty to make reasonable adjustments for disabled persons.

The duty to make reasonable adjustments comprises three requirements (s 20):

- **Provision, criterion or practice**

  Where a provision, criterion or practice puts a disabled person at a substantial disadvantage in relation to a relevant matter in comparison with persons who are not disabled, the requirement is that reasonable steps must be taken to avoid the disadvantage.

- **Physical features**

  Where a physical feature puts a disabled person at a substantial disadvantage in comparison with persons who are not disabled, the requirement is that reasonable steps must be taken to avoid the disadvantage.

- **Provision of auxiliary aid**

  Where a disabled person would, but for the provision of an auxiliary aid, be at a substantial disadvantage in comparison with persons who are not disabled, the requirement is that reasonable steps must be taken to provide the auxiliary aid.

A failure to comply with any of these requirements in respect of an individual is discrimination (s 21).

In each case a disabled person must be at a 'substantial disadvantage'. 'Substantial' is defined as 'more than minor or trivial'. The threshold is therefore relatively low.

3.6 Solicitors as service providers

3.6.1 Unlawful behaviour

Under Part 3 Equality Act 2010 the anti-discriminatory provisions of the Act are made applicable to those providing services to members of the public. A service provider is defined as a person concerned with the provision of services. A service provider can be an individual or a business. This includes solicitors as providers of legal services (and it includes all providers of legal services, even if unregulated (see **1.7**). There is no requirement that the provider receive payment for the services. Consequently, the Act also applies to solicitors providing free legal advice.

Under s 29 it is unlawful for a service provider:

- to discriminate or victimise:
  - by not providing the service
  - as to the terms on which the service is provided

- ○ by terminating the provision of the service, or
- ○ by subjecting the user of the service to any detriment.
- Or to harass the person to whom the service is provided.

In essence, people who have protected characteristics should not be discriminated against when using any service. The Act therefore protects the individual requiring the service. In the context of legal services this will be the client or prospective client. The Act applies to the *provision* of the service rather than the nature of the service. The protection applies to seeking the service, during the provision of the service and can extend to after the service has been provided.

Under s 29 it would be unlawful for a solicitor to discriminate against or harass a client because of a protected characteristic or victimise a client when providing legal services. Discrimination in this context could take the form of, for example, refusing to act for a client, providing legal services on less advantageous terms or terminating the retainer. The prohibition applies to all the protected characteristics except marriage/civil partnership and age, where the individual is under 18 years of age.

3.6.2 Vicarious liability

Under s 109 Equality Act 2010 acts done by an employee are treated as if done by the employer. This means that a firm may be held vicariously liable for the behaviour of an individual employee. This applies irrespective of the fact that the employee's acts were done without the firm's knowledge or approval. The individual remains liable whether or not the employer is found to be vicariously liable.

Vicarious liability only arises in respects of an act of discrimination which was committed by an employee in the course of their employment. There is a defence in that a firm will be able to avoid vicarious liability if it can show that they took such steps as were 'reasonable' to prevent the particular act of discrimination or acts of that description. However, those steps must have been taken before the discriminatory act occurred.

3.6.3 Making adjustments

Section 29 also imposes the duty to make adjustments. A service provider will be considered to have discriminated against a disabled person if they fail to comply with the duty to make reasonable adjustments. In relation to physical features (see **3.5**) the requirement is to take reasonable steps to avoid the disadvantage or to adopt a reasonable alternative method of providing the service. However, there is no requirement to fundamentally change the nature of the service being provided. The cost of making adjustments cannot be passed onto those using the service.

The duty is owed to 'disabled people generally'. The duty is imposed irrespective of whether the service provider is already providing services to disabled people. The provider is therefore required to anticipate the possibility of disabled people using its services and make appropriate adjustments, rather than waiting for a particular disabled person to encounter a problem or raise an issue. For example, a firm of solicitors is under a duty to take reasonable steps to make its office building wheelchair accessible even though none of its current clients use a wheelchair. The duty arises even if the service provider is unaware that an individual is disabled or is likely to suffer disadvantage. However, only an individual affected by the failure to make adjustments can bring a claim.

In assessing whether the adjustments are 'reasonable', various factors will be considered, including the cost of making the adjustment, the nature of the service being provided and the size of the firm.

3.6.4 Making a claim

A client can make a claim under the Act to the county court. Initially the burden of proof lies with the claimant to show a prima facie case of discrimination (s 136). The claimant must prove facts from which it could be inferred that discrimination has taken place. The burden then shifts to the defendant. If a prima facie case has been established the court must make a finding that there has been a breach of the legislation unless the defendant is able to prove otherwise.

The court can grant any remedy which the High Court could make in tort or judicial review cases. The usual remedy is damages. There is no limit on the damages that can be awarded. This may include financial loss, personal injury and compensation for injury to feelings. Claims in respect of services are usually limited to injury to feelings simply because the claimant has not suffered a financial or other loss. Damages may be aggravated if, for example, the defendant's behaviour has been malicious or oppressive. In rare cases damages may be exemplary. If the firm and the employee are both found to be liable, the claimant does not receive double compensation; they will be jointly liable for the amount of damages awarded by the court. The court may also grant other remedies, such as declarations or injunctions, if appropriate.

3.7 Solicitors as employers

3.7.1 Unlawful acts

Under Part 5 Equality Act 2010 the anti-discriminatory provisions of the Act are made applicable to the workplace. In basic terms, employees are protected from discriminatory behaviour at the hands of their employers. Employees in this context includes partners or those seeking partnership and members or prospective members of Limited Liability Partnerships.

The provisions of the Act apply to employers in their treatment of their employees or prospective and, in some cases, former employees. A firm of solicitors (or individual partners) will usually employ staff. Those who work for a firm of solicitors are therefore protected under the Act.

Under ss 39 and 40 an employer must not:

- discriminate against or victimise a prospective employee:
  - in the arrangements made for deciding to whom to offer employment
  - as to the terms on which employment is offered, or
  - by not offering employment.
- harass a person who has applied to it for employment
- discriminate against or victimise an employee:
  - as to the terms of employment
  - in the way it affords access to opportunities for promotion, transfer or training, or for receiving any other benefit, facility or service
  - by dismissing the employee, or
  - by subjecting the employee to any detriment.
- harass an employee.

Detriment is established if a reasonable employee would or might take the view that they had been disadvantaged in the circumstances in which they had to work. There is therefore no need for the claimant to prove some physical or financial consequences.

3.7.2 Vicarious liability

Vicarious liability for the acts of employees (see **3.6.2**) also applies in the context of employment.

3.7.3 Occupational requirements

An exception applies in the employment context which means that in some instances discrimination will not be unlawful. The exception applies where an employer is able to demonstrate that, because of the nature of the job, only people with a particular protected characteristic are able to do it. For example, in a Roman Catholic school it may be lawful to require stipulation that the head teacher must be a practising Roman Catholic. An employer will only be able to rely on the exception if they can show that the requirement is a proportionate means of achieving a legitimate aim. The exception is unlikely to be relevant to most firms of solicitors.

3.7.4 Making adjustments

Section 39 also imposes the duty to make adjustments for disabled employees or prospective employees. An employer will be considered to have discriminated against a disabled person if they fail to comply with the duty to make reasonable adjustments.

In contrast to service providers, employers are only required to make adjustments if they know or ought reasonably to know that the individual is disabled and likely to be disadvantaged. The duty is not anticipatory; it only applies to particular individuals. So, for example, a firm does not need to modify a recruitment process to accommodate the possibility of a disabled applicant. The duty arises when a disabled person applies or notifies the firm that they intend to do so.

The Government Legal Service v Brookes UKEAT 0302/16

The claimant, who suffered from Asperger's Syndrome, applied for a job as a trainee solicitor with the Government Legal Service Board. The first step in the recruitment process required all applicants to sit and pass an online multiple-choice test. The claimant asked to be able to sit the test in the form of short narrative written questions on the basis that her condition placed her at a disadvantage in attempting multiple-choice style questions. The claimant's request was refused. The claimant proceeded to attempt the multiple-choice test but did not pass. The Government Legal Service was found to have failed to make adjustments for the claimant in not giving her the opportunity to sit the test in a different format (and to have subjected the claimant to indirect discrimination and disability discrimination).

3.7.5 Making a claim

An employee or prospective employee can make a claim to the Employment Tribunal.

As a first step an employee or prospective employee who considers that they might have been discriminated against can submit questions to the employer to help determine whether they have a claim. The purpose of this step is to address the imbalance in employment cases where the employer alone is usually in possession of the information relating to the allegations of discrimination.

The employee will then have to participate in a conciliation process through the Advisory, Conciliation and Arbitration Service to see if the claim can be settled. Conciliation must be attempted before the Employment Tribunal will be prepared to accept the claim.

The Employment Tribunal can award unlimited compensation. Compensation is intended to put the employee in the position they would have been in if the wrong had not occurred. Usually the compensation in employment cases will be for financial loss (such as loss of earnings, loss of promotion, or loss of bonus), but injury to feelings can also be included. The Tribunal can also make declarations of the employee's rights or make a recommendation that the employer must take specified steps for the purpose of obviating or reducing the adverse effect on the employee of any matter to which the proceedings relate.

3.7.6 Preventing sexual harassment

With effect from 26 October 2024, s 40A Equality Act 2010 places employers under a positive duty to take reasonable steps to prevent the sexual harassment of their employees in the course of their employment. This is separate from an employer's obligations in relation to harassment related to a protected characteristic. The preventative duty is both anticipatory and ongoing and requires the employer to be proactive. What constitutes 'reasonable' steps is judged objectively taking account of the employer's circumstances.

3.8 Barristers

Under s 47 Equality Act 2010 special provisions apply to barristers.

Barristers are protected from discrimination by members of chambers or clerks of chambers in which they are tenants or pupils. Those who have applied for tenancy or pupillage are also protected.

Barristers are also protected from discriminatory treatment at the hands of the solicitors instructing them. Section 47(6) provides that:

A person must not, in relation to instructing a barrister:

(a) discriminate against a barrister by subjecting the barrister to a detriment;

(b) harass the barrister;

(c) victimise the barrister.

3.9 Positive action

In certain circumstances the Act allows positive action to be taken in an attempt to address the disadvantages suffered by those who share a protected characteristic. There is no requirement for positive action to be taken; instead the Act provides that if such action is taken it will not be unlawful. The point is that action taken to address the disadvantages suffered by those who share a protected characteristic may result in less favourable treatment of those who do not share that protected characteristic. However, if certain requirements are met the positive action will be lawful.

Section 158 contains a general provision allowing positive action which will apply to solicitors both as service providers and employers. There are two requirements which must be met for the action to be considered lawful.

The first requirement is that the firm must reasonably think that:

* persons who share a protected characteristic suffer a disadvantage connected to the characteristic; or

* persons who share a protected characteristic have needs that are different from the needs of those who do not share it; or

* participation in an activity by persons who share a protected characteristic is disproportionately low.

The firm must be able to show some basis for its belief, such as a survey of its clients or an analysis of the make-up of its workforce.

The second requirement is that the action taken by the firm is a proportionate means of achieving one of the following aims:

* enabling or encouraging persons who share the protected characteristic to overcome or minimise that disadvantage; or

- meeting those needs; or

- enabling or encouraging persons who share the protected characteristic to participate in that activity.

Positive action can take a variety of forms. It could include, for example, a firm tailoring some of its services to meet the requirements of a particular group or providing specific training to some of its employees.

A similar provision is contained in s 159 Equality Act 2010, but it is restricted to the areas of recruitment and promotion. Section 159 applies where an employer reasonably thinks that persons with a particular protected characteristic are disadvantaged or disproportionately under-represented. In the context of recruitment and promotion, the employer can treat a person with the protected characteristic more favourably than others who do not share that protected characteristic. However, this is only permitted where the person with the relevant characteristic is 'as qualified as' the others. Qualification in this context is not restricted to having passed particular examinations, but instead relates to the overall suitability of the individual for the job or promotion. In practice, it is said that an employer can make use of s 159 in a 'tie-breaker' situation.

✪ Example

> A firm has a vacancy for a position as an assistant solicitor. The firm receives 20 applications and decides to draw up a shortlist of five applicants for interview. The first four applicants are selected. For the fifth place there are two applicants of equal merit, one of whom belongs to a particular ethnic group, the other applicant is not. The firm has identified that individuals from this ethnic group are under-represented amongst its qualified staff. To address this the firm gives the fifth shortlist place to the applicant from the ethnic group.
>
> The firm's action is lawful under s 159. The other applicant would not have any redress under the Act.

Sections 158 and 159 are not intended to allow 'positive discrimination', which is the practice of giving an advantage to groups which are often treated unfairly because of a protected characteristic. For example, if in the above example the firm decided to shortlist all applicants from the ethnic group irrespective of their suitability for the job, such action would be unlawful.

3.10 Overlap with professional conduct

Paragraph 7.1 of the SRA Code of Conduct for Solicitors, RELs and RFLs requires a solicitor to keep up to date with and follow the law and regulation governing the way they work. 'Law and regulation' in this context obviously includes the Equality Act 2010. The SRA therefore expects those it regulates to be aware of and comply with their obligations under the Act.

Paragraph 7.1 places a personal responsibility on the individual, but firms should provide appropriate training for its staff on the Act. This is good management and will also help the firm to establish that it took steps to prevent discriminatory acts by its employees and thereby avoid vicarious liability (see **3.6.2**).

In many cases a failure to comply with the Act will of itself give rise to additional professional conduct issues. Discriminatory acts, by their very nature, diminish trust and confidence in the profession and therefore breach SRA Principle 2. A solicitor who fails to comply with the Act is therefore likely to be subject to separate disciplinary action. The sanctions imposed may be severe. The SRA Enforcement Strategy states:

> We will also consider behaviour which harms an individual's personal autonomy and dignity and treat fundamental rights to privacy and non-discriminatory treatment as at the higher end of seriousness, irrespective of any financial or other harm.

The Act establishes minimum legal requirements. However, solicitors are expected to do much more than comply with the Act. Discrimination is also dealt with separately under both the SRA Code of Conduct for Solicitors, RELs and RFLs and the SRA Code of Conduct for Firms. Both Codes start with the statement in Paragraph 1.1:

> You do not unfairly discriminate by allowing your personal views to affect your professional relationships and the way in which you provide your services.

In part, Paragraph 1.1 reflects the prohibitions under the Act, but it also extends beyond the Act. In Paragraph 1.1 the term 'discrimination' is not restricted to the meaning given to it under the Act. So discriminatory behaviour which is not unlawful under the Act (for example because it is not based on a protected characteristic or because it is based on a disability which does not fall within the narrow definition in s 6) may nevertheless breach Paragraph 1.1 and result in disciplinary action.

SRA Principle 6 requires a solicitor to act in a way that encourages equality, diversity and inclusion. This clearly goes far beyond a direction not to discriminate. It places a positive requirement on the solicitor to ensure that their actions encourage equality, diversity and inclusion. These are wide and distinct concepts. In very simple terms:

> Equality – treating people fairly

> Diversity – encouraging and valuing people with a broad range of different backgrounds, knowledge, skills, and experiences

> Inclusion – acceptance and encouraging everyone to participate and contribute

The importance the SRA places on Principle 6 is evident from its Guidance on Equality, Diversity and Inclusion:

> We expect you to take the necessary steps to run your business or carry out your role in a way that encourages equality of opportunity and respect for diversity. We expect you to be inclusive in your approach to everything you do.

Principle 6 also extends to a solicitor's conduct outside practice. For example, a solicitor who, in a personal capacity, expresses racist views on social media is likely to be in breach.

Solicitors come into contact with a variety of people during their working day: clients, judiciary, work colleagues, counsel, expert witnesses etc. Treating those people fairly, with dignity and respect, is part and parcel of upholding the reputation of the profession. Firms must also be mindful of these requirements in all dealings with their staff. The SRA expects firms to look after the wellbeing of their staff and to protect them from bullying, harassment, discrimination and victimisation. The SRA also encourages those who have experienced or witnessed such behaviour to report it to the SRA (SRA Guidance – Workplace environment: risks of failing to protect and support colleagues).

Firms should put policies and procedures in place to further equality, diversity and inclusion. Indeed, a failure to have such policies may in itself be a breach of Principle 6. Such policies and procedures should also extend to protecting staff and supporting their wellbeing. A determination to uphold these values should be embedded in the culture of the firm and the attitudes of the people that work within it.

The principles of equality, diversity and inclusion do not only direct how a solicitor should interact with others; they also drive the development of the profession as a whole. The SRA considers the development of a diverse profession to be a hugely important aspect of its role. Indeed, one of the regulatory objectives set out in the Legal Services Act 2007 is 'encouraging an independent, strong, diverse and effective legal profession'. The SRA expects individual firms to play their part by, for example, monitoring, reporting and publishing data on the diversity of its workforce (Paragraph 1.5 of the SRA Code of Conduct for Firms) and, if necessary, putting measures in place to improve diversity.

Summary

- The following characteristics are protected under the Act:
  - race
  - religion and belief
  - sex
  - sexual orientation
  - age
  - disability
  - gender reassignment
  - marriage/civil partnership
  - pregnancy and maternity.

- The Act outlaws certain forms of discrimination including:
  - direct discrimination
  - indirect discrimination
  - disability discrimination
  - victimisation
  - harassment.

- There is a duty to make reasonable adjustments for disabled people.

- Discrimination is outlawed in certain circumstances including in the provision of services and the workplace.

- The Act overlaps with a solicitor's professional conduct responsibilities.

Sample questions

Question 1

A secretary working in a firm of solicitors is subjected to a number of unwanted sexual advances by a solicitor working in the same firm. The firm has never provided training for its employees on the Equality Act 2010. The secretary makes a complaint to the firm's senior partner. The senior partner says that the firm was completely unaware of the solicitor's behaviour. The senior partner promises to speak to the solicitor in question and insist that the behaviour stops. Despite this the solicitor continues to make sexual advances to the secretary. In view of the solicitor's behaviour the secretary is now contemplating making a claim to the Employment Tribunal.

Which of the following best describes the likely outcome of such a claim?

A   The solicitor's behaviour will not be considered unlawful because it amounts to normal workplace banter.

B   The solicitor and the firm will be liable for harassment.

C   The firm is not liable for the solicitor's behaviour because it did not know about the behaviour.

D   The firm alone will be liable for harassment.

E   The secretary will not be entitled to damages because they have not suffered any financial loss.

Answer

Option B is correct. The solicitor's behaviour amounts to harassment under the Act (option A is wrong). The solicitor's behaviour occurred in the course of their employment and so the firm will also be vicariously liable even though the firm did not know about the behaviour; accordingly, option C is wrong. It is highly unlikely that the firm will be able to show that it took reasonable steps to prevent the behaviour because it had not provided training and its response to the complaint was inadequate. If the firm is found liable, the individual employee cannot escape liability (option D is wrong). Finally, option E is wrong, as even though the secretary has not suffered a financial loss, they may be awarded damages for injury to feelings.

Question 2

A solicitor's brother is going through an acrimonious divorce. The whole family is finding the divorce proceedings very upsetting. One evening, having drunk a considerable amount of alcohol, the solicitor goes onto social media and makes various sexist remarks about his brother's wife. The solicitor's firm is not acting in the divorce.

Which of the following best describes the repercussions of the solicitor's actions under the Equality Act 2010?

A   The solicitor's actions amount to direct discrimination.

B   The solicitor's actions amount to victimisation.

C   The solicitor's actions are not unlawful under the Equality Act 2010 and do not breach the rules of professional conduct.

D   The solicitor's actions are not unlawful under the Equality Act 2010 but they are likely to breach the rules of professional conduct.

E   The solicitor's actions amount to indirect discrimination.

Answer

Option D is correct. The Equality Act 2010 only makes discrimination unlawful in certain contexts (eg in the provision of legal services and in the workplace). As the comments were made outside those contexts they do not amount to unlawful discrimination under the Act. The SRA Principles apply to a solicitor's private life. Making sexist comments is likely to place the solicitor in breach of Principle 2 and Principle 6.

Question 3

A client instructs a large commercial firm of solicitors in connection with a medical negligence claim. At the first meeting the solicitor conducting the case hands the client a standard leaflet explaining the firm's complaints procedure. The client looks at the leaflet for the first time later that day. The client, who has learning difficulties, contacts the firm and asks to have the leaflet provided in 'Easy Read' format. The firm has not previously given any consideration to the provision of information in an 'Easy Read' format. The client is told that the firm does not produce its leaflets in 'Easy Read' format.

Which of the following best describes how the firm's duty to make reasonable adjustments under the Equality Act 2010 applies in this situation?

A   The firm has acted unlawfully in not providing the client with the leaflet in 'Easy Read' format at the initial interview.

B   Now that the firm is aware of the client's disability, it must provide the client with the leaflet in 'Easy Read' format without delay.

C   Now that the firm is aware of the client's disability, it should provide the leaflet in 'Easy Read' format at the client's expense.

D   It is not reasonable to expect the firm to provide the leaflet in 'Easy Read' format.

E   The firm has not breached its duty under the Equality Act 2010 but is likely to be in breach of its professional conduct obligations.

Answer

Option A is correct. The duty to make reasonable adjustments in the context of the provision of services is anticipatory. The firm should have anticipated the need for clients with some disabilities to have the leaflet in 'Easy Read' format and to have had the leaflet produced accordingly. The client's need for adjustments should have been established by the solicitor at the first interview and the client given the leaflet in the correct format. Given the situation that has arisen, the firm should provide a leaflet in the correct format without delay, but option B is not the best answer because the firm's duty had already arisen; it is not dependent on knowledge of the client's disability. Option C is wrong as the cost of making adjustments cannot be passed on to the disabled person. Given the size of the firm, the importance of providing clients with information about complaints (Paragraph 8.3 of the SRA Code for Solicitors, RELs and RFLs requires written information to be provided at the outset) and the fact that the firm has chosen to present that information in leaflet form, it would not be unreasonable to expect the firm to also produce the leaflet in 'Easy Read' format (accordingly, option D is wrong). Finally, option E is not the best answer here. While the firm is likely to be in breach of its professional conduct obligations (eg SRA Principle 6 and Paragraph 8.6 of the SRA Code of Conduct for Solicitors, RELs and RFLs), it is also in breach of the requirements under the Equality Act 2010.

4 Financial Services

SQE1 syllabus

This chapter will enable you to achieve the SQE1 Assessment Specification in relation to Functioning Legal Knowledge concerned with Legal Services:

- The regulatory role of the Solicitors Regulation Authority.

- Overriding legal obligations.

- The financial services regulatory framework, including authorisation and how it applies to solicitors' firms.

- Recognition of relevant financial services issues, including the identification of specified investments, specified activities and relevant exemptions.

- Application of the Financial Services and Markets Act 2000 and related secondary legislation to the work of a solicitor.

- Appropriate sources of information on financial services.

Note that for SQE1, candidates are not usually required to recall specific case names or cite statutory or regulatory authorities. However, in this chapter the following may be referred to in the SQE1 assessments: Financial Services and Markets Act 2000, including s 19 (general prohibition) and s 327 (exemption for professional firms); SRA Financial Services (Scope) Rules; SRA Financial Services (Conduct of Business) Rules. Cases are provided for illustrative purposes only.

Learning outcomes

By the end of this chapter you will be able to apply relevant core legal principles and rules appropriately and effectively, at the level of a competent newly qualified solicitor in practice, to realistic client-based and ethical problems and situations in the following areas:

- The structure of financial services regulation.

- The regulation of solicitors in carrying out financial services work.

4.1 Introduction

The financial service industry comprises firms and individuals that advise on, sell and arrange financial products and services. For most people it is an alien world and yet almost every individual will be forced to engage with it at some point, for example when taking out an insurance policy or becoming a member of a pension scheme. At these moments the customer or consumer will be highly dependent on the expertise of others in making the right financial decisions. For the customer or consumer the stakes are high: the wrong financial product or the wrong decision could spell financial ruin. It is therefore not surprising that the provision of financial services is highly controlled and regulated with the basic aim of ensuring that such services are provided properly by those appropriately qualified to do so.

Financial services work is not mainstream for most solicitors. However, a solicitor may encounter financial services from time to time, for example:

(a) in conveyancing, if a client needs help in finding a mortgage and a supporting package, which could include a life insurance policy;

(b) in probate, when the executors sell off the deceased's assets;

(c) in litigation, if helping a successful client to invest damages just won;

(d) in company work, in making arrangements for a client to buy or sell shares in a company, and also in arranging corporate finance;

(e) in family work, if arrangements have to be made on a divorce in respect of endowment life policies and/or a family business;

(f) in tax planning or portfolio management, for a private client including trustees.

In all cases a solicitor should first consider their professional conduct obligations. Under SRA Principle 7, a solicitor must act in the client's best interests. A solicitor cannot act in the client's best interests unless the solicitor is competent to act in the area concerned. Additionally, Paragraph 3.2 of the SRA Code of Conduct for Solicitors, RELs and RFLs provides that the service provided by a solicitor must be competent. Therefore, a solicitor should not undertake financial services work of any nature unless the solicitor has sufficient expertise in that field.

Even if possessing sufficient expertise, a solicitor will be subject to the same legislation that applies throughout the financial sector and so will also have to consider what that legislation permits them to do. Many activities in connection with investments are subject to regulation under the Financial Services and Markets Act 2000 (FSMA 2000) and, for example, to give advice on these, or even to make arrangements for clients to acquire or dispose of them, may require the solicitor to be authorised to carry out that activity. To do this without authority could involve the commission of a criminal offence. Therefore, when handling a matter in which investments are involved, even if only peripherally, a solicitor needs to take great care before advising and assisting such clients.

This chapter looks at:

• source materials

• financial services regulatory structure

• the need for authority

• the general prohibition

• exemption for professional firms

• SRA Financial Services (Conduct of Business) Rules

- consumer credit activity
- insurance distribution
- financial promotions restriction

4.2 Source materials

The main piece of legislation in this area is FSMA 2000. However, the Act itself provides only a general framework, and the detail is in secondary legislation (mainly Orders in Council made by the Treasury), for example:

(a) Financial Services and Markets Act 2000 (Regulated Activities) Order 2001, SI 2001/544 (RAO 2001);

(b) Financial Services and Markets Act 2000 (Professions) (Non-Exempt Activities) Order 2001, SI 2001/1227;

(c) Financial Services and Markets Act 2000 (Financial Promotion) Order 2005, SI 2005/1529 (FPO 2005).

Materials on financial services work include:

(a) the SRA Financial Services (Scope) Rules (Scope Rules);

(b) the SRA Financial Services (Conduct of Business) Rules (COB Rules).

4.3 Financial services regulatory structure

The regulation of financial services is mainly in the hands of two bodies established under the Financial Services Act 2012: the Financial Conduct Authority and the Prudential Regulation Authority. In addition the Financial Policy Committee (a committee of the Bank of England) is responsible for monitoring the stability of the whole UK financial system.

4.3.1 The Financial Conduct Authority (FCA)

The FCA is an independent regulator which is accountable to Parliament. The FCA regulates firms providing financial services and financial markets in the UK. Most firms providing financial services must be authorised to do so by the FCA under FSMA 2000. The FCA sets rules and standards which firms must abide by and has the power to take action against those who fail to do so. As the name indicates, the FCA is primarily concerned with 'conduct regulation', or how firms behave.

The FCA's overarching strategic objective is to ensure that financial markets function well. The FCA is also set the following operational objectives under FSMA 2000:

(a) securing an appropriate degree of protection for consumers;

(b) protecting and enhancing the integrity of the UK financial system;

(c) promoting effective competition in the interests of consumers in the market, including for regulated financial services.

4.3.2 The Prudential Regulation Authority (PRA)

The PRA is part of the Bank of England. The PRA regulates those businesses which manage significant financial risks, namely banks, building societies, insurers, credit unions and major investment firms. The PRA sets policies and maintains a supervisory role in respect of the firms it authorises. As the name indicates, the PRA is primarily concerned with 'prudential regulation' which is aimed at ensuring that financial risks are managed sensibly and that the firms undertaking those risks remain well-managed and financially secure. The general objective set for the PRA in FSMA 2000 is 'promoting the safety and soundness' of the firms it authorises.

Some firms will be dual-regulated, ie subject to regulation by both the FCA and the PRA.

4.4 The need for authority

A primary aim of FSMA 2000 is to ensure that financial services are only provided by those who are properly qualified and regulated. It achieves this by restricting the provision of most types of financial services to those who have been authorised to do so (or are subject to an exemption) and imposing penalties on those who provide such services without proper authorisation (or exemption). Most firms of solicitors are not authorised to provide financial services. Solicitors do, however, encounter financial services in their mainstream work (for example, in those circumstances described in **4.1**), and so in most instances the solicitor's task is to make sure that they do not stray into doing anything that requires authorisation. The solicitor therefore needs to know what they can and cannot do under FSMA 2000.

The two restrictions imposed by FSMA 2000 of greatest relevance to solicitors are:

(a) carrying out a regulated activity (the general prohibition);

(b) making a financial promotion (the financial promotions restriction).

4.4.1 The general prohibition

Section 19 FSMA 2000 provides that: 'No person may carry on a regulated activity in the UK unless authorised or exempt.'

Authorised persons are persons with permission granted by the appropriate regulator (the FCA) under FSMA 2000.

Carrying out a regulated activity without authorisation or exemption is a criminal offence under s 23 FSMA 2000. The penalty on conviction is up to two years' imprisonment or unlimited fine. Breach of s 19 may also render unenforceable any resulting agreement which has as a party to it the person who contravened s 19, or made with an authorised person carrying on a regulated activity.

4.4.2 The financial promotions restriction

Under s 21 FSMA 2000 an unauthorised person cannot engage in a financial promotion. Again, the FCA is the regulator. It is a criminal offence under s 25 FSMA 2000 to make an unauthorised financial promotion.

4.5 The general prohibition

The main provision of relevance to solicitors is the general prohibition in s 19 FSMA 2000. As stated above, the basic aim of the prohibition is to ensure that financial advice and assistance is only provided by those who are both properly qualified and regulated.

Businesses cannot carry out certain activities, known as 'regulated activities', unless authorised by the appropriate regulator or subject to a an exemption. In the case of a solicitors' firm, the appropriate regulator will be the FCA. FSMA 2000 contains an exemption for professional firms. If certain conditions are satisfied, under the exemption, a professional firm will be able to carry on certain regulated activities without breaching the general prohibition in s 19.

In short, if a firm wishes to engage in regulated activities, it must be authorised by the FCA or fall within the exemption for professional firms.

Under s 22 FSMA 2000 a regulated activity is defined as an activity of a specified kind that is carried on by way of business and relates to a specified investment or property of any kind. Hidden within this definition are a number of tests.

4.5.1 The four tests

In order to determine if an activity is regulated there are four tests:

(a) Are you in business?

(b) Is there a specified investment (see **4.5.3**), or does the specified activity relate to information about a person's financial standing or administering a benchmark?

(c) Is there a specified activity (see **4.5.4**)?

(d) Is there an exclusion (see **4.5.5**)?

The particular activities and investments are specified by the Treasury in the RAO 2001. Information about a person's financial standing includes providing, or advising upon, credit reference and credit information services (FSMA 2000, Sch 2). The term 'benchmark' is defined in s 22(6A) FSMA 2000. Benchmarks are used in markets to help set prices, measure performance, work out amounts payable under financial contracts or the value of financial instruments.

4.5.2 The business test

To qualify as a regulated activity it must be carried on by way of business. Whilst at the margins determining whether a person is 'in business' may be a complex issue, in the vast majority of cases it will be obvious. A solicitor giving advice etc in that capacity as part of their practice will be 'in business'.

4.5.3 Specified investments

A specified investment is one specified as such in RAO 2001. The qualifying criteria for each type of investment are detailed, but broadly specified investments include:

(a) company stocks and shares (but not shares in the share capital of open-ended investment companies or building societies incorporated in the UK);

(b) debentures, loan stock and bonds;

(c) government securities, such as gilts;

(d) unit trusts and open-ended investment companies (OEICs);

(e) insurance contracts (including life policies and annuities);

(f) regulated mortgage contracts (most residential mortgages);

(g) home reversion/home purchase plans (the former enables a homeowner to sell the whole or a proportion of their property to a finance provider in order to raise funds, and then become a tenant of the property, whilst the latter serves the same purpose as a mortgage but is structured in a way that is compliant with Islamic law);

(h) deposits (these would include cash ISAs and sums of money held in bank or building society accounts). However, the only specified activity relating to these investments is 'accepting deposits', which is mainly carried out by banks and building societies. The main specified investment activities set out in **4.5.4** do not apply to deposits. Sums received by solicitors acting in the course of their business are exempt under RAO 2001;

(i) credit agreements (an agreement whereby a solicitor allows a client time to pay is exempt provided that the number of repayments does not exceed 12, the payment term does not exceed 12 months and the credit is provided without interest or other charges).

Investments that will not be relevant include:

(a) interests in land;

(b) certain National Savings products.

4.5.4 Specified investment activities

A specified activity is one specified as such in RAO 2001. In relation to specified investments, these include (but are not limited to):

(a) dealing as agent;

(b) arranging;

(c) managing;

(d) safeguarding;

(e) advising;

(f) lending money on/administering a regulated mortgage contract.

There are also specified activities that are very particular in their scope, such as establishing, operating or winding up a collective investment scheme or personal pension scheme.

4.5.4.1 Dealing as agent

This involves buying, selling, subscribing for or underwriting the investments when a solicitor is dealing on behalf of a client (ie rather than on the solicitor's own account) and commits that client to transactions. For example, selling shares on behalf of a client pursuant to a financial order made on divorce.

4.5.4.2 Arranging

Solicitors will have many clients whose transactions involve investments (eg endowment policies in conveyancing, unit trusts and shares in probate). The solicitor will very often be involved as the contact between the client and the life company, or the client and the stockbroker. It is in this context that the solicitor may be 'arranging'.

4.5.4.3 Managing

Managing requires active participation beyond the mere holding of investments and applies only to 'discretionary management' (ie involving the exercise of discretion). This investment activity will be most common in firms that undertake probate and trust work, where the solicitor is acting as trustee or personal representative (PR).

4.5.4.4 Safeguarding

This involves safeguarding and administering investments belonging to a client. This is also particularly relevant for firms which undertake probate and trust work.

4.5.4.5 Advising

This involves giving advice to a person in their capacity as an investor on the merits of buying, selling, subscribing for, or underwriting an investment. Advice must be about a specific investment; generic advice is outside the scope of FSMA 2000. Therefore a solicitor can, if they have the knowledge, advise a client on the respective merits of investing in shares rather than making a deposit with a bank, but if the solicitor advises the client to buy shares in a particular company, say Tesco, this will be a regulated activity.

⭐ *Example*

Hiran, a solicitor, has recently managed to secure a large settlement for his client, Bethany, in respect of a recent litigation matter. Bethany tells Hiran that she wishes to invest the settlement money in buying shares in a local company, and asks Hiran which company she should invest in.

Referring to the four-stage test, Bethany is seeking Hiran's advice in his capacity as a solicitor, so Hiran is 'in business'. Shares are a specified investment, and Hiran has been asked to advise on the purchase of these shares – advising is a specified investment activity. Therefore if Hiran gives this advice he will breach the 'general prohibition' under s 19 FSMA 2000, which is a criminal offence, unless Hiran can take advantage of an exclusion or exemption (see below).

4.5.5 Exclusions

There are various exclusions set out in RAO 2001. The effect of an exclusion is that an act which would otherwise be a regulated activity is no longer regarded as such. If an exclusion applies to a particular activity a solicitor is carrying out, the solicitor does not need to be authorised for that particular transaction. Those exclusions likely to be relevant to solicitors include:

(a) introducing;

(b) using an Authorised Third Party;

(c) acting for an execution-only client;

(d) acting as trustee or personal representative;

(e) the 'professional/necessary' exclusion;

(f) the 'takeover' exclusion.

Each exclusion is only applicable to certain of the specified activities.

4.5.5.1 Introducing

This exclusion only applies to the activity of arranging. For the exclusion to apply the solicitor must simply introduce the client to an authorised person and then have no further role in this aspect of the client's matter. If the solicitor retains any ongoing role, such as acting as a means of communication between the client and the authorised person, then the exclusion cannot be relied upon.

This exclusion will not apply if the transaction relates to an insurance contract.

4.5.5.2 Authorised third persons – the ATP exclusion

This exclusion applies to the activities of dealing as agent and arranging.

The exclusion applies where the transaction is to be entered into based on the advice of an ATP, ie a person authorised by the FCA. Here the solicitor retains an ongoing role in the transaction, but it is clear that the financial advice is being provided by the ATP.

A solicitor cannot rely on this exclusion if the solicitor receives from any person other than the client any pecuniary reward (eg commission) or other advantage arising out of the client entering into the transaction, for which the solicitor does not account to the client.

This exclusion will not apply if the transaction relates to an insurance contract.

Although this exclusion does not apply to advising, the practical result of using an ATP is that a solicitor will not be engaged in the activity of advising. The advice is being provided by the ATP, not by the solicitor.

4.5.5.3   The execution-only client exclusion

This exclusion applies to the activities of dealing as agent and arranging.

There is an exclusion similar to the ATP exclusion. However, rather than the positive requirement that the transaction is entered into on the advice of the ATP, the requirement here is negative – ie advice has not been sought from the solicitor.

This exclusion applies where the client, in their capacity as an investor, is not seeking and has not sought advice from the solicitor as to the merits of the client's entering into the transaction (or, if the client has sought such advice, the solicitor has declined to give it but has recommended that the client seek such advice from an authorised person).

There is the same restriction in respect of commissions and contracts of insurance.

4.5.5.4   Trustees or personal representatives

This exclusion applies to arranging, managing, safeguarding and advising fellow trustees and/or beneficiaries. It also applies to lending money on, or administering, a regulated mortgage contract.

This exclusion has limitations. It is available to a solicitor acting as a trustee or PR, and not to a solicitor acting *for* a trustee or PR. However, the exclusion does apply if a member of the firm is a trustee or PR but the activity is actually carried out by other members of the firm. The exclusion does not apply if the solicitor is remunerated for what the solicitor does 'in addition to any remuneration he receives as trustee or personal representative, and for these purposes a person is not to be regarded as receiving additional remuneration merely because his remuneration is calculated by reference to time spent'. For managing and safeguarding, the exclusion is also not available if the solicitor holds themselves out as providing a service comprising managing or safeguarding.

The Law Society's guidance provides that this exclusion will not apply to contracts of insurance. It also does not apply to taking up or pursuing insurance distribution (see **4.10**).

4.5.5.5   Activities carried on in the course of a profession or non-investment business – the 'professional/necessary' exclusion

This applies to advising, arranging, safeguarding and dealing as agent.

There is an exclusion if the activity is performed in the course of carrying on any profession or business and may reasonably be regarded as a necessary part of other services provided in the course of that profession or business, ie where it is not possible for the other services to be provided unless the regulated activity is also provided. Examples of where this exclusion may apply include: when acting on the acquisition of a company, giving advice on the merits of buying it and arranging for the acquisition of its shares; or, in probate work, arranging for the sale of all of the assets to pay Inheritance Tax.

However, the exclusion does not apply if the activity is remunerated separately from the other services. Further, if the activity consists of taking up or pursuing insurance distribution (see **4.10**), this exclusion is not available.

4.5.5.6   Activities carried on in connection with the sale of a body corporate – the takeover exclusion (or body corporate exclusion)

This exclusion applies to arranging, advising and dealing as agent.

The exclusion will apply to a transaction to acquire or dispose of shares in a body corporate (other than an OEIC), or for a transaction entered into for the purposes of such an acquisition or disposal, if:

(a) the shares consist of or include 50% or more of the voting shares in the body corporate; and

(b) the acquisition or disposal is between parties each of whom is a body corporate, a partnership, a single individual or a group of connected individuals.

It is possible to add the number of shares being acquired by a person to those already held by them in order to determine whether the 50% limit has been achieved. A 'group of connected individuals' is a single group of people, each of whom is or will be a director or manager of the company being sold, or a close relative of any such director or manager, or person acting as trustee for any of the above persons.

Even if the above criteria are not met, eg the number of shares acquired is less than 50%, but the object of the transaction may nevertheless reasonably be regarded as being the acquisition of day-to-day control of the affairs of the body corporate, the exclusion still applies.

This is an extremely valuable exclusion for the corporate department where a client is seeking to take over, or sell its interest in, a company, whether public or private.

This exclusion does not apply to advising on, arranging, or dealing as an agent in respect of buying or selling contracts of insurance.

4.5.5.7 Summary table

The table below summarises the specified investment activities to which the exclusions apply.

Specified activity	Applicable exclusions
Dealing as agent	• ATP • Execution-only • Professional/necessary • Takeover
Arranging	• Introducing • ATP • Execution-only • Professional/necessary • Acting as trustee/PR • Takeover
Advising	• Professional/necessary • Acting as trustee/PR • Takeover
Managing	• Acting as trustee/PR
Safeguarding	• Professional/necessary • Acting as trustee/PR

> ⭐ **Example**
>
> *Natalie is a solicitor. Natalie is approached by Byron, who owns 100% of the share capital in Merron Ltd. Byron wishes to sell 75% of these shares to his son.*
>
> *Referring to the four tests, Byron is seeking Natalie's advice and assistance in her capacity as a solicitor, so Natalie is 'in business'. Shares are a specified investment, and in dealing with the matter Natalie will be carrying out specified investment activities (eg advising and arranging). Therefore, Natalie will need to rely on an exclusion or exemption to avoid breaching s 19 FSMA 2000 and committing a criminal offence.*
>
> *Here the transaction concerns the transfer of more than 50% of Merron Ltd, and so she can rely on the takeover exclusion. Therefore Natalie may complete this work without breaching the general prohibition.*

4.6 Exemption for professional firms – s 327 exemption

Under the s 327 exemption professional firms are able to carry out certain regulated activities without breaching the general prohibition in s 19 provided certain conditions are met. The exemption only applies to a firm which is regulated and supervised by a designated professional body (a DPB), such as the SRA.

In essence, the effect of falling within s 327 is that the general prohibition does not apply to a regulated activity carried out by the firm; in other words the firm is exempt from the general prohibition. The exemption is very important for solicitors. The majority of solicitors' firms are not authorised by the FCA. Therefore, in order to engage in financial services work, most solicitors will have to be able to rely on the exemption. A firm which satisfies the requirements of s 327 is sometimes referred to as an 'exempt professional firm'.

The exemption makes a special provision for firms that do not carry out mainstream financial services but which undertake regulated activities in the course of other work, eg conveyancing, personal injury and trust work. The effect is that firms authorised by the SRA can carry out certain regulated activities (exempt regulated activities) without being regulated by the FCA if the firm can meet the conditions in s 327 FSMA 2000.

Under s 327, the general prohibition in s 19 FSMA 2000 will not apply to a regulated activity carried on by a firm of solicitors if the following conditions are met:

(a) the firm must not receive from a person other than its client any pecuniary or other advantage arising out of the activity for which it does not account to its client;

(b) the manner of providing 'any service in the course of carrying on the activities must be incidental to the provision' by the firm of professional services, ie services regulated by the SRA;

(c) the firm must only carry out regulated activities permitted by the DPB;

(d) the activities must not be prohibited by an order made by the Treasury, or any direction made by the FCA under s 328 or s 329;

(e) the firm must not carry on any other regulated activities.

4.6.1 'Pecuniary or other advantage'

If the firm wishes to take advantage of the s 327 exemption then it must account for any such pecuniary advantage to its client. This is mirrored by Paragraph 4.1 of the SRA Code of Conduct for Solicitors, RELs and RFLs and Paragraph 5.1 of the SRA Code of Conduct for Firms.

4.6.2 'Incidental'

There are two 'incidental' tests: a specific test and a general test.

The 'specific' test relates to the particular client concerned. Under the SRA Financial Services (Scope) Rules, the relevant regulated activity must arise out of, or be complementary to, the provision of a particular professional service to a particular client. The firm could not, therefore, carry out a regulated activity in isolation for a client; the relevant regulated activity must 'arise out of' or be 'complementary to' some other service being provided by it. This other service must not be a regulated activity but must be a 'professional', ie legal, service (eg in corporate work, giving legal advice, drafting documents or dealing with a regulatory matter; or in probate work, winding up the estate or giving tax advice). It follows that the professional service being provided to the client should be the primary service, and the regulated activity should be 'incidental' or 'subordinate' to the provision of the professional service. Note also that both the professional service and the regulated activity must be supplied to the same person. Therefore, in a probate matter, where the probate client is the executor, advice to a beneficiary under the will would not satisfy this test.

To satisfy the 'general' test of being incidental, the activities carried out by the firm which would otherwise be regulated cannot be a major part of the firm's activities. For example, a firm will be ineligible if its income from investment business is half or more of its total income. Further factors are:

(a) the scale of regulated activity in proportion to other professional services provided;

(b) whether and to what extent the exempt regulated activities are held out as separate services; and

(c) the impression given of how the firm provides those activities, for example through advertising its services.

4.6.3 Permitted regulated activities only

In its regulatory role the SRA has published the SRA Financial Services (Scope) Rules and the SRA Conduct of Business (COB) Rules. Firms must comply with the requirements prescribed by these rules at all times when seeking to use this exemption.

The Scope Rules set out the scope of the activities that firms can carry out under the professional exemption. For example:

(a) A solicitor or firm must not carry on any activity that is specified in an order made by the Treasury under s 327(6) FSMA 2000. Examples of such activities include recommending to a client to dispose of any rights the client has under a personal pension scheme and advising a client to become a member of a particular Lloyd's syndicate. Further prohibited activities are set out in the Scope Rules themselves, such as creating or underwriting a contract of insurance.

(b) If a firm wishes to undertake insurance distribution activities (see **4.9**), it must notify the SRA, be registered in the Financial Services Register and have appointed an insurance distribution officer who will be responsible for such activities.

(c) There are further restrictions in the context of corporate finance and credit-related regulated financial services activities.

4.6.4 Not prohibited

The Treasury has set out, in FSMA 2000 (Professions) (Non-Exempt Activities) Order 2001, a list of activities that cannot be provided by professional firms under the s 327 exemption. The activities that are most relevant to solicitors are incorporated into the Scope Rules.

The FCA also has power, under s 328, to issue directions limiting the application of the exemption in respect of different classes of persons or different descriptions of regulated activities.

4.6.5 No other regulated activities

The s 327 exemption cannot be used by firms which are authorised by the FCA. For example, a firm could be authorised by the FCA concerning defined regulated activities. Such a firm could not use s 327 for any other 'non-mainstream' regulated activities.

4.7 SRA Financial Services (Conduct of Business) Rules

The COB Rules regulate the way in which a firm may undertake financial services under the professional exemption. The COB Rules apply only when the firm is carrying out an exempt regulated activity; they do not apply if the firm is not carrying out a regulated activity at all.

4.7.1 Status disclosure (Rules 2.1 and 2.2)

A firm must provide clients with certain information concerning the status of the firm. For example, the firm must confirm to the client that it is not authorised by the FCA, and explain that complaints and redress mechanisms are provided through the SRA and the Legal Ombudsman. Any information that is provided under these rules must be given in a manner that is clear, fair and not misleading.

4.7.2 Best execution (Rule 3.1)

A solicitor must act in the best interests of the client (SRA Principle 7). Therefore, the firm must carry out transactions for clients as soon as possible unless it reasonably believes that it is in the client's best interest not to.

4.7.3 Transactions (Rules 4.1 and 4.2)

The firm must keep records of:

(a) instructions from clients to carry out transactions; and

(b) instructions to third parties to carry them out.

4.7.4 Commissions (Rule 5.1)

The firm must keep records of commissions received in respect of regulated activities and how those commissions were dealt with.

4.7.5 Execution-only clients (Rule 7.1)

Where a firm acts for an execution-only client (see **4.5.5.3**) and the investment concerned is a retail investment product (eg life policies, unit trusts, stakeholder and personal pension schemes), it must send a letter to the client confirming that the client is not relying on the advice of the solicitor, and the firm must keep a copy of this letter.

This rule would apply, for example, when the packaged retail investment product is a contract of insurance. Here the 'execution only' exclusion would not apply, and therefore the solicitor would have to rely on the exemption for professional firms (see **4.6**) (and therefore comply with the COB Rules).

4.7.6 Insurance distribution activities (COB Rules, Part 3)

There are stringent requirements which must be met when any insurance distribution activities are carried out. For example, all information about insurance distribution must be communicated to clients in a way that is clear, fair and not misleading, and information on the nature of the remuneration received in relation to a contract of insurance must be provided to the client before the conclusion of the initial contract.

4.8 Consumer credit activity

Consumer credit activity (for example, credit brokerage, debt collecting under a consumer credit or hire agreement, debt advice and debt management or administration) is a relatively new type of regulated activity for the purposes of s 22 FSMA 2000. The activities (known as credit-related regulated financial services activities) are set out in Part 2 and Part 3A RAO 2001.

Accordingly, solicitors carrying out such activities will need to be authorised by the FCA to carry out this business, or ensure that the activities fall within the s 327 exemption (see **4.7**). Representing a client in a litigation matter which has arisen from a consumer credit or hire agreement is not a credit-related activity for these purposes.

A solicitor could be carrying out a credit-related activity by virtue of the way in which the solicitor accepts the payment of their fees, including allowing a client time to pay. However, such an arrangement will be regarded as an exempt agreement under RAO 2001 if all of the following conditions apply:

(a) the number of repayments does not exceed 12;

(b) the payment term does not exceed 12 months; and

(c) the credit is provided without interest or other charges.

In most other cases, such arrangements are likely to be covered by the s 327 exemption (in which case Part 4 of the COB Rules will apply).

4.9   Insurance distribution

The definition of 'insurance distribution' in RAO 2001 includes:

> The activities of advising on, proposing or carrying out other work preparatory to the conclusion of contracts of insurance, of concluding such contracts, or of assisting in the administration and performance of such contracts, in particular in the event of a claim ...

'Contracts of insurance' are defined widely, and include life policies (eg endowment policies), car insurance, buildings and contents insurance, defective title insurance, after-the-event legal insurance and annuities.

Rights under contracts of insurance are specified investments (see **4.5.3**), and in addition to the specified investment activities discussed in **4.5.4**, there are other specified activities set out in the RAO 2001 which specifically cover insurance contracts, such as assisting in the administration and performance of a contract of insurance. Law firms carrying out probate, property and personal injury work are most likely to be involved in such activities. Whatever the type of contract of insurance involved, if a solicitor assists a client in obtaining one, even if all the solicitor does is to introduce the client to an insurance broker, the solicitor will be carrying out a specified activity. Similarly, if a solicitor is involved in an insurance claim against an insurance company, this will also be caught. All of these activities involve insurance distribution. There is a detailed definition of 'insurance distribution activity' in the SRA Glossary.

Given that the main exclusions will almost certainly not apply to insurance distribution, the firm will have to rely on the s 327 exemption (see **4.6**), seek authorisation from the FCA, or rely on the limited exceptions available for insurance distribution activities (which are beyond the scope of this manual).

✪ *Example*

Franklin, a solicitor, is acting for Sanjay on purchasing a commercial property. Sanjay needs to obtain defective title insurance. Franklin is to arrange this for Sanjay.

Using the four tests, Franklin is providing this service to Sanjay in his capacity as a solicitor and so he is 'in business'. Contracts of insurance are a specified investment and arranging is a specified investment activity. Therefore Franklin needs to rely on an exclusion or exemption to avoid breaching s 19 FSMA 2000 and committing a criminal offence.

However, none of the exclusions will apply here. Therefore, in order to arrange the insurance, Franklin must use the s 327 exemption. Here, arranging the insurance is incidental to Franklin dealing with the property transaction. If Franklin's firm can comply with the other conditions outlined above (eg the COB and Scope Rules) then Franklin will be able to arrange the defective title insurance without breaching the general prohibition.

4.10 Financial promotions restriction

Section 21 FSMA 2000 provides that a person must not, in the course of business, communicate an invitation or inducement to engage in an investment activity unless the promotion has been made or approved by an authorised person or it is exempt. This is known as the financial promotion restriction.

In s 21, reference to the making of a promotion by an 'authorised' person means authorised by the FCA. Reference to the promotion having been 'approved by an authorised person' means by an authorised person that has been granted 'approver permission' from the FCA to approve the financial promotions of unauthorised persons.

In essence, s 21 is directed at protecting individuals making investments who are likely to be influenced by financial promotions when deciding how and where to invest. Financial products are by their very nature highly complex, and so the 'lay' individual will inevitably rely on the claims or representations made in promotional material. The aim of s 21 is therefore to ensure that financial promotions are only made or approved by those who are properly qualified and regulated.

In much the same way as for the general prohibition in s 19 FSMA 2000, a series of tests can be applied in order to determine whether a communication by an unauthorised person falls foul of the financial promotion restriction, namely:

- Is a communication being made?
- Is the communication an invitation or inducement?
- Is there an investment activity?
- Is the communication made in the course of business?
- Does the communication fall within one of the exemptions?

If the answer to the first four questions is 'yes', an unauthorised person cannot communicate the promotion unless it has been approved by an authorised person or it falls within one of the exemptions.

4.10.1 Communication

Communication involves giving material or transmitting material to the recipient. All types of communication will be caught by the restriction, including face to face, emails, letters and websites. Guidance from the FCA says that to communicate requires a person to take an active step to make the communication. That said, the action need not be direct. For example, simply leaving copies of a document where it is reasonable to assume that people will pick up copies and may seek to act on them (for example, brochures left in the solicitor's waiting room) will amount to communication of the content of that document.

The FPO 2005 distinguishes between different types of communications: real time and non-real time, and solicited and unsolicited. A real time communication is one made in the course of a personal visit, telephone conversation, or other interactive dialogue. A non-real time communication is any other communication (eg made by letter, email or brochure). A real time communication is solicited where it is made in the course of a personal visit, telephone conversation or other interactive dialogue that is initiated by or takes place in response to an express request from the recipient. An unsolicited real time communication is any other real time communication that is not solicited. In essence, the regime is aimed to provide the greatest protection where individuals are at their most vulnerable, namely when in receipt of an unsolicited real time communication.

4.10.2 Invitation or inducement

The financial promotion regime applies to a communication that is an invitation or inducement to engage in investment activity. An invitation will directly invite a person to take a step that will result in them engaging in investment activity. An inducement is a significant step in seeking to persuade or incite someone to engage in investment activity.

The terms 'invitation' and 'inducement' are not defined in FSMA 2000. Guidance from the FCA says that s 21 regulates communications that have a promotional element. In other words, such communications include a degree of persuasion or incitement rather than simply providing information about an investment and/or its associated risks. Consequently, a communication that does not have any element of persuasion or incitement will not fall within s 21. The FCA states that the essential elements of an invitation or an inducement are that it must both have the purpose or intent of leading the recipient to engage in investment activity and be promotional in nature, 'so it must seek, on its face, to persuade or incite the recipient to engage in investment activity'. The test is an objective one.

4.10.3 Investment activity

'Investment activity' is defined in s 21(8) as entering into a 'controlled activity' or exercising any rights conferred by a 'controlled investment'. Schedule 1 FPO 2005 contains a list of controlled activities and controlled investments. Again, the requirements are detailed, but examples of controlled activities are 'advising on' and 'managing' certain investments; examples of controlled investments include shares and insurance contracts. Whilst there is a degree of overlap, the FPO 2005 is wider than the lists of specified investments and specified investment activities in RAO 2001.

4.10.4 Business

Again, 'acting in the course of business' is not defined in FSMA 2000. The FCA's view is that it should be given its ordinary meaning.

4.10.5 Exemptions

The FPO 2005 sets out a long list of exemptions. In essence those types of communication considered to present less risk (eg solicited real time communications) may be able to take advantage of an exemption. Provided that all the requirements of the exemption are met, an unauthorised person will be able to communicate the financial promotion without it first being approved by an authorised person.

Examples of exemptions which may be of relevance to the work of solicitors are:

4.10.5.1 One-off promotions (FPO 2005, arts 28/28A)

One-off, non-real time communications and solicited real time communications are exempt under the FPO 2005, art 28 if certain conditions are satisfied. Basically the communication must be one that is personal to the client.

One-off, unsolicited real time communications are exempt under art 28A, provided the solicitor believes on reasonable grounds:

(a) that the client understands the risks associated with engaging in the investment activity to which the financial promotion relates; and

(b) that, at the time of the communication, the client would expect to be contacted by the solicitor in relation to that investment activity.

4.10.5.2 Introducers (FPO 2005, art 15)

A solicitor may make any real time communication in order to introduce a client to an authorised person who carries on the controlled activity to which the communication relates, provided:

(a) the solicitor is not connected to (eg a close relative of) the ATP;

(b) the solicitor does not receive other than from the client any pecuniary reward or other advantage arising out of making the introduction; and

(c) the client is not seeking and has not sought advice from the solicitor as to the merits of engaging in investment activity (or, if the client has sought such advice, the solicitor has declined to give it, but has recommended that the client seeks such advice from an authorised person).

Summary

Regulated activity

In order to determine if an activity is regulated there are four tests:

- Are you in business?
- Is there a specified investment?
- Is there a specified investment activity (or an activity related to information about a person's financial standing or administering a benchmark)?
- Is there an exclusion?

Specified investments

These include:

- shares (but not shares in the share capital of an open-ended investment company or building society incorporated in the UK);
- debentures;
- gilts;
- unit trusts and OEICs;
- contract of insurance;
- regulated mortgages;
- home reversion/home purchase plans;
- deposits.

Investments that will not be relevant include:

- interests in land;
- most National Savings products.

Specified investment activities

These include:

- dealing as agent;
- arranging;
- managing;
- safeguarding;
- advising.

Exclusions

These include:

- introducing;
- ATP;

- execution-only;
- trustee/PR;
- professional/necessary;
- takeover.

Exempt regulated activities

A firm not authorised by the FCA should pay attention to:

- FSMA 2000;
- RAO 2001;
- any rules made by the FCA;
- SRA Scope Rules.

Conditions set out in the FSMA 2000, the RAO 2001 and the Scope Rules overlap.

The main conditions for claiming the s 327 exemption are:

- the activity must arise out of, or be complementary to, the provision of a particular professional service to a particular client;
- the manner of provision by the firm of any service in the course of carrying out the activities is incidental to the provision by the firm of professional services;
- the firm must account to the client for any reward or other advantage which the firm receives from a third party;
- the Scope Rules do not prohibit the firm using the exemption.

Conduct of Business Rules

The SRA COB Rules apply only when the firm is carrying out an exempt regulated activity; they do not apply if the firm is not carrying out a regulated activity at all.

The SRA COB Rules cover:

- best execution;
- records of transactions;
- records of commissions;
- letters to execution-only clients;
- insurance distribution activities;
- credit-related regulated financial services activities.

Financial promotions

There are five questions:

- Is a communication being made?
- Is the communication an invitation or inducement?
- Is there an investment activity?
- Is the communication made in the course of a business?
- Does the communication fall within an exemption?

Sample questions

Question 1

A solicitor acts for a client who is a director of a private limited company. The client also owns 60% of the share capital in the company. The client intends to retire and plans to sell the entire shareholding to a fellow director of the company. The client asks the solicitor to advise on the sale and to prepare and negotiate all the necessary documentation. The solicitor's firm is not authorised by the Financial Conduct Authority to carry out regulated activities under the Financial Services and Markets Act 2000.

Which of the following best explains why the solicitor is likely to be able to advise and act as the client requests?

A   Because shares in private companies are not specified investments.

B   Because the solicitor would not be carrying out a specified investment activity.

C   Because the solicitor can rely on the exemption for professional firms.

D   Because the solicitor would be giving generic advice.

E   Because the solicitor can rely on the 'takeover' exclusion.

Answer

Option E is correct. The client is seeking advice and assistance from the solicitor who is 'in business'. Shares in a private company are a specified investment (option A is wrong), and in acting as the client requests the solicitor will be carrying out the specified investment activities of advising and arranging (option B is wrong). The solicitor will need to rely on an exclusion or exemption to avoid breaching s 19 FSMA 2000.

The takeover exclusion applies to a transaction to acquire or dispose of shares in a body corporate if the shares include 50% or more of the voting shares and is between parties each of whom is a body corporate, a partnership, a single individual or a group of connected individuals. Here the client wishes to sell his 60% shareholding in the company to a fellow director, so the takeover exclusion requirements are satisfied.

Advising on the sale of shares would not be considered generic advice (option D is wrong).

Option C is wrong because the exemption for professional firms is of no relevance as the solicitor will not be carrying out a regulated activity (and the requirements of s 327 would not be met).

Question 2

A solicitor has just finished acting for a client in a personal injury case. The client has decided to buy a flat using the damages that the client has received in the case. The client has identified a number of possible flats to buy. The solicitor knows nothing about the property market; nevertheless the client asks the solicitor to advise on which flat would provide the best investment. The solicitor's firm is not authorised by the Financial Conduct Authority to carry out regulated activities under the Financial Services and Markets Act 2000.

What would be the position if the solicitor gave the advice as requested?

A   Criminal proceedings may be brought against the solicitor.

B   Disciplinary proceedings may be brought against the solicitor.

C   The solicitor will have complied with their duty to act in the best interests of the client.

D   Criminal proceedings may be brought against the firm, but not against the solicitor personally.

E   The solicitor will have complied with their duty to act with integrity.

Answer

Option B is correct. Land is not a specified investment and so in giving the advice the solicitor will not be committing an offence under FSMA 2000. However, the solicitor is not competent to give the advice. Therefore, the solicitor is in breach of Paragraph 3.2 of the Code of Conduct for Solicitors, RELs and RFLs and disciplinary proceedings may be brought against them. Giving advice when not competent to do so would not constitute acting with integrity nor acting in the client's best interests.

Question 3

A solicitor has been acting for a client in a litigation matter. The case recently concluded with the client being awarded £3 million in damages. The client asks the solicitor for advice on investing this money in debentures and bonds. The solicitor lacks sufficient expertise to advise the client and so the solicitor refers the client to an independent financial adviser. After the client has seen the adviser, the client asks the solicitor to arrange the purchase of the investments that the adviser has recommended. The adviser pays the solicitor £50 commission, which, without reference to the client, the solicitor decides to retain.

Has the solicitor breached the general prohibition in the Financial Services and Markets Act 2000?

A   No, because the solicitor will be able to rely on the exemption for professional firms.

B   No, because the client has taken advice from an authorised third person.

C   No, because the transaction did not involve a specified investment.

D   Yes, because the solicitor lacked competence.

E   Yes, because the solicitor received a pecuniary reward.

Answer

Option E is correct. Debentures and bonds are specified investments (option C is wrong) and the solicitor has engaged in the specified activity of arranging. Ordinarily the solicitor would be able to rely on the ATP exclusion, but this is not available where the solicitor receives commission and fails to account to the client; accordingly option B is wrong. Option A is wrong because the financial services were not incidental on the facts and so the requirements in s 327 are not met. Finally, option D is wrong as 'competence' does not influence whether the act amounts to a regulated activity (but is a professional conduct issue).

5 Money Laundering

SQE1 syllabus

This chapter will enable you to achieve the SQE1 Assessment Specification in relation to Functioning Legal Knowledge concerned with Legal Services:

- The regulatory role of the Solicitors Regulation Authority.
- Overriding legal obligations.
- Purpose and scope of money laundering legislation including the international context.
- Due diligence requirements.

Note that for SQE1, candidates are not usually required to recall specific case names or cite statutory or regulatory authorities. Cases are provided for illustrative purposes only.

Learning outcomes

By the end of this chapter you will be able to apply relevant core legal principles and rules appropriately and effectively, at the level of a competent newly qualified solicitor in practice, to realistic client-based and ethical problems and situations in the following areas:

- The nature of money laundering.
- Solicitors' obligations under anti-money laundering legislation.
- Due diligence.

5.1 Introduction

Money laundering is the process by which criminals seek to alter or 'launder' their proceeds of crime so that it appears that these funds come from a legitimate source.

For example, a criminal may be in possession of stolen money and instructs a number of intermediaries each to invest a relatively small proportion of the money. The investments can later be sold, and the criminal then appears to be in possession of the proceeds of a legitimate transaction. Such transactions can become highly complex, making it very difficult for investigators to follow the 'audit trail' and track the funds.

By the very nature of their work solicitors constantly deal with transactions and handle money on behalf of their clients. Consequently solicitors are particular targets for criminals in their efforts to launder their proceeds of crime or give their criminal activities the appearance of legitimacy.

This chapter looks at:

- the relevance of money laundering for solicitors
- the purpose of the Regulations
- the application of the Regulations
- risk assessment
- policies, controls and procedures
- internal controls
- client due diligence
- training
- record keeping
- economic crime
- the UK financial sanctions regime

5.2 The relevance of money laundering for solicitors

Anti-money laundering legislation is part of the general law applicable to all. However, it has a particular relevance and significance for solicitors. Money laundering regularly features in the SRA Risk Outlook (see **2.3**) as a key risk facing the profession.

There will inevitably be a handful of solicitors who are knowingly and deliberately complicit in money laundering. The focus here is not on them; they are criminals and the criminal law will deal with them in any event. Instead, the focus is on ordinary solicitors who may be targeted, and at risk of being used, by criminals. These solicitors will be caught up in money laundering if they do not take sufficient care.

Those engaged in money laundering will often seek to use a solicitor to facilitate their criminal activities. Some criminals, for example, will simply wish to instruct a solicitor because it lends an air of respectability to their activities. However, the susceptibility of solicitors to money laundering largely arises from the type of work they do. Almost all solicitors handle money for their clients and others and, depending on the nature of the firm, that money may be held in other jurisdictions. Solicitors also conduct the type of transactions which criminals view as ideal methods for laundering money.

It is generally accepted that money laundering involves three distinct stages:

Placement: money from criminal activity is introduced into the financial system.

Layering: the money is distanced from the criminal activity by passing it through a number of parties or transactions.

Integration: the money is integrated back into the financial system and the criminal is now in possession of 'laundered' money.

A solicitor can become involved at any stage. However, there are some areas of solicitors' work that are thought to present a particular risk:

(a) Company and trust work

Both companies and trusts can be complex legal entities. Therefore, when setting them up money can be hidden behind complicated structures and layers of ownership. Solicitors can also sometimes be involved in the ongoing management of companies and trusts and so be used by criminals to create the appearance of respectability for their activities.

(b) Use of a client account

Passing money through a firm's client account is an obvious way of 'swapping' illicit money for clean money.

⭐ Example

Mark is a solicitor specialising in commercial work. Mark is instructed by Henry in the purchase of a business. The day after the initial interview, Henry telephones to say that he has been called away because his mother is seriously ill and so he has placed £750,000 in the firm's client account to ensure that, if necessary, the purchase can go ahead in his absence.

Three weeks later Henry telephones Mark and says that he has decided not to go ahead with the purchase. Henry says that it will help his cash flow if, rather than returning the £750,000 to him direct, it is transferred to a company that Henry owns abroad. Mark makes the transfer.

Henry could be a criminal and the £750,000 represents the proceeds of his crimes. If that is the case, Mark has enabled the illicit money to be swapped for legitimate money apparently originating from a firm of solicitors and then being transferred out of the jurisdiction.

(c) Real estate

Acting for a client in the purchase of a property is said to be the classic area of a solicitor's work at risk of money laundering. By definition, money has to pass through the firm's client account to enable the transaction to proceed. At the end of the transaction the criminal is in possession of an asset, often appreciating in value, which can be sold in order to produce 'legitimate' proceeds plus profit. Buyer and seller may, or may not, be complicit in the illegal activity.

⭐ Example

Nicola instructs Jasmin, a solicitor, to act for her in the purchase of a house. The purchase price of the house is £500,000. Nicola says that she does not need a mortgage to buy the house as she has just received an inheritance. Nicola transfers £500,000 into the firm's client account to complete the purchase.

Inexplicably the seller drops the price to £400,000 and the purchase completes. Nicola instructs that the surplus of funds which the firm is holding for her should be paid to a business associate in settlement of a debt. Jasmin pays the surplus to the business associate.

It may be that the £500,000 represents the proceeds of crime and the seller is complicit in the criminal activity. If this is the case Jasmin has enabled Nicola to acquire a legitimate asset for later sale and allowed the surplus to be 'cleansed' by passing through the firm's client account and transferred to a third party.

(d) Sham litigation

Litigation is not an area of work that at first sight appears to be at risk from money launderers. However, such a risk may arise in the context of sham litigation. Sham litigation is where a fake dispute is manufactured in order that the legal outcome of that dispute (by court or or settlement) can be used as a front for the transfer of money/assets.

⭐ *Example*

Frank is a solicitor specialising in commercial litigation. Frank is instructed by Rosen Ltd to issue a claim against a foreign company. Frank duly issues the claim. However the foreign company does not defend the claim and judgement is entered in default.

The foreign company immediately pays the sum due to Frank's firm. Frank pays the money onto Rosen Ltd.

Rosen Ltd and the foreign company may have been complicit in engaging in sham litigation for the purpose of transferring illicit funds from abroad into the UK. Frank has assisted in that process.

5.3 The purpose of the Regulations

The regulatory requirements are to be found in the Money Laundering, Terrorist Financing and Transfer of Funds (Information on the Payer) Regulations 2017 (SI 2017/692) ('the Regulations').

As the name indicates the Regulations also cover terrorist financing. In essence terrorist financing involves the use of funds (whether or not the proceeds of crime) for illicit political purposes. The UK, in common with many other jurisdictions, combines measures against money laundering with measures against terrorist financing because both activities involve criminals entering into transactions with the intent of hiding the origins and/or destinations of the funds. This chapter concentrates on money laundering as this is the type of activity which solicitors are most likely to encounter in practice.

Crime has become a global phenomenon. The ease with which money and people can now pass from one country to another means that money laundering is also global in nature. Such activity demands an international response. The Financial Action Task Force is an inter-governmental body established as a consequence of concern at the growing incidence of money laundering around the world. The Regulations (together with other legislation) is the UK's response to the recommendations made by the Financial Action Task Force that countries should introduce their own laws to meet international objectives.

As with all legislation in this area the Regulations are intended to disrupt serious crime (including terrorism) by inhibiting criminals' ability to reinvest or benefit from the proceeds of crime. As upholders of justice and the rule of law solicitors should naturally be concerned to stop crime. However, the Regulations codify the steps which those who are at risk of coming up against money launderers (sometimes referred to as 'gatekeepers') should be expected to take in order to protect society as a whole.

The Regulations require systems and procedures to be put in place with a view to preventing money laundering and/or ensuring that such behaviour comes to the attention of the appropriate authorities for investigation. The approach is essentially risk based to ensure that the more significant measures are targeted at those situations which carry the higher risk. A failure to comply with the Regulations may be a criminal offence or incur civil penalties depending on the nature of the failure.

The Legal Sector Affinity Group publishes guidance for solicitors (and others) on compliance with the Regulations and other anti-money laundering legislation. The guidance is approved by HM Treasury.

5.4 The application of the Regulations

The Regulations apply to 'relevant' persons acting in the course of businesses carried out in the UK. This includes 'independent legal professionals' (reg 8), defined in reg 12 as:

> a firm or sole practitioner who by way of business provides legal or notarial services to other persons, when participating in financial or real property transactions ....

Trust or company service providers, tax advisers and insolvency practitioners are also included. The definition of 'relevant' persons will encompass many of the activities undertaken by solicitors, and therefore most firms will be subject to the Regulations. However, this will not always be the case; 'pure' litigation, for example, is outside the scope of the Regulations. Where an activity falls outside the scope of the Regulations, a solicitor is nevertheless still subject to the Proceeds of Crime Act 2002 (see **Chapter 6**) and must comply with all relevant professional conduct requirements.

The SRA has a supervisory role in respect of anti-money laundering under the legislation. There is a requirement for the 'beneficial owners, officers or managers' of the firm and sole practitioners to apply to the SRA for approval under the Regulations. Approval must be granted unless the applicant has been convicted of a 'relevant offence' (a long list of offences which fall within this definition is set out in Sch 3 and includes offences under previous money laundering legislation, the Terrorism Act 2006 and any offence which has deception or dishonesty as one of its components). Acting without such approval is a criminal offence and may result in imprisonment, a fine or both (reg 26).

In addition to the requirements under the Regulations, as a matter of professional conduct firms must have in place structures, arrangements, systems and controls that ensure compliance with regulatory and legislative requirements (Paragraph 2.1(a) SRA Code of Conduct for Firms) and must identify, monitor and manage material risks to the business (Paragraph 2.5 SRA Code of Conduct for Firms). These requirements include action needed to prevent the firm being used for money laundering or terrorist financing.

5.5 Risk assessment

A firm is required to take appropriate steps to identify and assess the risk of the firm being used for money laundering (reg 18). This will entail a firm-wide risk assessment to include risk factors relating to, for example, the services offered by the firm and how they are delivered, the nature of the firm's clients and the industries in which they operate.

The SRA monitors compliance and carries out a risk assessment across legal services. An individual firm's risk assessment must take account of the SRA's own assessment of the risks within the sector as a whole.

A risk assessment is a fundamental requirement and the starting point for all anti-money laundering activities within the firm. The SRA may ask to see a firm's risk assessment. The SRA takes a proactive approach and has indicated its determination to take enforcement action against a firm where the risk assessment is inadequate or where the firm does not have any risk assessment at all in place.

The Government's National Risk Assessment published in 2020 specifies the services provided by law firms most likely to be targeted by money launderers: trust and company services, conveyancing and client account services (see **5.2**). Firms need to ensure that their risk assessment addresses the risks in these areas.

A firm is required to keep an up-to-date written record of all of the steps it has taken in terms of the risk assessment.

5.6 Policies, controls and procedures

A firm is required to establish and maintain written anti-money laundering policies, controls and procedures (proportionate to its size and nature and approved by its senior management) to mitigate and manage effectively the money laundering and terrorist financing risks identified in its risk assessment (reg 19). This will include risk management practices, how the firm conducts client due diligence, the firm's reporting and record-keeping systems, policies put in place when new technology is adopted and in relation to complex, unusually large or unusual patterns of transactions which have no apparent economic or legal purpose.

5.7 Internal controls

A firm must appoint a 'nominated officer' (often referred to as the Money Laundering Reporting Officer or MLRO) to receive reports from within the firm concerning any instances of suspected money laundering and to liaise, if necessary, with the National Crime Agency (NCA) (reg 21(3)). In addition, a firm must appoint a Money Laundering Compliance Officer (MLCO) if this is appropriate having regard to the size and nature of the firm (reg 21(1)(a)). In practice most firms will appoint a MLCO who will act as the SRA's main point of contact on anti-money laundering issues. The roles of MLCO and nominated officer can be fulfilled by the same individual.

In addition to the above, a firm is required to adopt two further internal controls:

(a) The screening of relevant employees prior to and during the course of their employment to assess their skills, knowledge, conduct and integrity. This relates to employees whose work in the firm is relevant to compliance with the Regulations or who otherwise contribute towards the identification, prevention and detection of money laundering and terrorist financing (reg 21(1)(b)).

(b) Establishing an independent audit function to examine, evaluate, make recommendations and monitor the firm's policies, controls and procedures adopted to comply with the Regulations (reg 21(1)(c)).

A firm must also establish and maintain controls which enable it to 'respond fully and rapidly' to enquiries from law enforcement as to whether it maintains, or has maintained during the past five years, a business relationship with any person and the nature of that relationship (reg 21(8)).

5.8 Client due diligence

5.8.1 The requirement for due diligence

Subject to limited exceptions, firms carrying out relevant business are obliged to obtain verification of the identity of each of their clients (referred to as 'customer due diligence' in the Regulations). The need to verify the client's identity arises in a number of circumstances including the following (reg 27):

(a) where the client and solicitor agree to form a business relationship;

(b) carrying out an occasional transaction (ie one not carried out as part of a business relationship) that amounts to a 'transfer of funds' (essentially any transaction at least partially carried out by electronic means on behalf of a payer through a payment service provider, for example, a credit transfer) exceeding €1,000;

(c) carrying out an occasional transaction that amounts to €15,000 or more, whether the transaction is executed in a single operation or in several operations which appear to be linked;

(d) where the solicitor suspects money laundering or terrorist financing;

(e) where the solicitor doubts the veracity or adequacy of documents or information supplied to verify the client's identity.

The verification (as set out in reg 28) is required as soon as possible after first contact and must take place before a business relationship is established or the carrying out of the transaction (reg 30). However, a solicitor may verify the identity of the client during the establishment of a business relationship if:

(a) there is little risk of any money laundering or terrorist financing occurring;

(b) it is necessary not to interrupt the normal conduct of business; and

(c) the identity is verified as soon as practicable after contact is first established.

However, if the solicitor is unable to complete the client due diligence in time, the solicitor cannot:

(a) carry out a transaction with or for the client through a bank account; or

(b) establish a business relationship or carry out a transaction otherwise than through a bank account,

and in such circumstances the solicitor must also terminate any existing business relationship and consider making a disclosure to the NCA (reg 31).

The steps which a solicitor must take in order to verify the identity of the client varies according to the type of client involved and the risk of money laundering.

5.8.2 Standard due diligence

Standard due diligence will apply to most clients. The solicitor is obliged to verify the identity of the client on the basis of 'documents or information in either case obtained from a reliable source which is independent of the person whose identity is being verified' and to take reasonable measures to understand the ownership and control structure of non-natural persons such as trusts and companies (reg 28).

For natural persons, evidence of identity may be based on documents such as passports and photocard driving licences. Guidance for the legal sector (from the Legal Sector Affinity Group and approved by HM Treasury) considers it good practice to have either:

(a) one government document which verifies the person's name, address and date of birth; or

(b) a government document which verifies the person's full name, plus supporting documents which verify the person's name and date of birth.

Ideally the solicitor should have sight of the originals of such documents. However, it is permissible to rely on copies when this can be justified based on an assessment of the risks involved in doing so.

For non-limited liability partnerships, it will be necessary to obtain information on the constituent individuals who make up the partnership. However, where partnerships are well-known, reputable organisations with long histories in their industries and with substantial public information about them, the Law Society's guidance advises that it should be sufficient to obtain their name, registered or trading address and nature of business.

For companies, it is necessary to verify the existence of the company. The standard identifiers are:

(a) its name;

(b) its company number or other registration; and

(c) the registered office address and principal place of business (if different).

Unless it is a company listed on a regulated market, reasonable measures are to be taken to obtain and verify the law to which it is subject, its constitution or other governing documents and the names of the board of directors or other senior persons responsible for its operations (reg 28).

The firm must also collect proof of registration or an excerpt from the relevant register before establishing a business relationship with a UK company or limited liability partnership. Firms should be assisted in this regard by the obligation placed on a 'UK body corporate' (which includes listed and unlisted companies and limited liability partnerships) to provide certain information on request when it forms a business relationship with a firm (and other persons to whom the Regulations apply), which includes the information listed above (reg 43). The legal sector guidance advises that it may also be appropriate to consider whether the person providing the instructions on behalf of the company has the authority to do so.

In addition, where simplified due diligence does not apply it will be necessary to consider the identity of beneficial owners.

Beneficial owners

A solicitor must verify the identity of any 'beneficial owner' where the beneficial owner is not the client. The definition of a beneficial owner varies depending on the nature of the client.

In the case of companies, reg 5(1) defines a beneficial owner as:

(a) any individual who exercises ultimate control over the management of the body corporate;

(b) any individual who ultimately owns or controls (in each case whether directly or indirectly), including through bearer share holdings or by other means, more than 25% of the shares or voting rights in the body corporate; or

(c) an individual who controls the body corporate.

This regulation does not apply to a company listed on a regulated market. It does apply to UK limited liability partnerships.

⭐ *Example*

> *A Co Ltd instructs a firm of solicitors. The solicitors will have to obtain documentary confirmation of the name, number, registered address and the other information set out in reg 28. This can be obtained by carrying out a company search at Companies House. However, the solicitors also need to identify any 'beneficial owner' of the company.*
>
> *If Mr Smith owns 50% of the shares, Mr Jones owns 30% of the shares and Mr McConnell owns the remaining 20%, Smith and Jones will be the beneficial owners.*

It may be that, instead of being owned by individuals, the client company is owned by a parent company. The legal sector guidance states that a risk-based decision should be taken as to whether to make further enquiries. However, it is common for law firms to seek to identify the beneficial owners of any parent company up to and including the ultimate parent entity.

In the case of a partnership (other than a limited liability partnership), reg 5(3) defines a beneficial owner as any individual who:

(a) ultimately is entitled to or controls (whether the entitlement or control is direct or indirect) more than a 25% share of the capital or profits of the partnership, or more than 25% of the voting rights in the partnership; or

(b) otherwise exercises control over the management of the partnership (ie the ability to manage the use of funds or transactions outside of the normal management structure and control mechanisms).

In the case of a trust, beneficial owner means each of the following (reg 6(1)):

(a) the settlor;

(b) the trustees;

(c) the beneficiaries;

(d) where the individuals (or some of the individuals) benefiting from the trust have not been determined, the class of persons in whose main interest the trust is set up, or operates;

(e) any individual who has control over the trust, ie one who has power (whether exercisable alone, jointly with another person or with the consent of another person) under the trust instrument or by law, for example, to add or remove a person as beneficiary, or to appoint or remove trustees.

As a trust does not have legal personality, the trust itself will not be the client, and so where a solicitor advises any individual client in relation to a trust, the solicitor will be required to understand who the other beneficial owners of the trust are, as defined above.

Whilst generally the beneficiaries of a trust will be individuals, they may at times be a company. If this is the case, it is necessary to apply reg 6(4) to determine the beneficial owners of the company in question.

In the case of other arrangements or entities, for example unincorporated associations and foundations, beneficial owner means those individuals who hold equivalent or similar positions to those set out above in reg 6(1).

5.8.3 Simplified due diligence

Simplified due diligence is permitted where a firm determines through an individual risk assessment that the business relationship or transaction presents a low risk of money laundering or terrorist financing, taking into account the risk assessment. The factors to be taken into account in determining whether a client or transaction poses a lower risk include whether the client is a company listed on a regulated market and the location of the regulated market and where a client is established and does business (reg 37(3)). However, the Regulations make it clear that the presence of one or more of the factors set out does not necessarily indicate that there is a lower risk in a particular situation.

The solicitor must obtain evidence that the transaction and the client are eligible for simplified due diligence. The exact verification required depends on the identity of the client, and the solicitor will not necessarily need to obtain information on the beneficial owners. For example, for a well-known plc listed in the UK, the solicitor must obtain confirmation of the company's listing on the Stock Exchange.

5.8.4 Enhanced due diligence

Enhanced due diligence is required where there is something about the arrangement or transaction which creates a high risk of money laundering. The Regulations set out a list of circumstances in which enhanced due diligence must be carried out (reg 33). These include where:

(a) the case has been identified as one where there is a high risk of money laundering or terrorist financing in the firm's risk assessment or in the information made available by the SRA and the Law Society;

(b) the client or the counter-part to the transaction is in a high-risk third country (as listed on the Financial Action Task Force website);

(c) the client has provided false or stolen identification documentation or information and the solicitor has decided to continue dealing with the client;

(d) the client is a politically exposed person (PEP), or a family member or known close associate of a PEP;

(e) a transaction is complex or unusually large, or there is an unusual pattern of transactions, or the transactions have no apparent economic or legal purpose;

(f) in any other situation where there is a higher risk of money laundering or terrorist financing. In determining this, there is a wide range of factors for a firm to take into account, for example whether the business relationship is conducted in unusual circumstances (such as where a solicitor has not met the client face to face), or payments will be received from unknown or associated third parties.

In these situations, a solicitor must take measures, as far as reasonably possible, to examine the background and purpose of the transaction and consider whether it is appropriate, for example, to obtain further independent verification of the client's or beneficial owner's identity or more detail on the ownership, control structure and financial situation of the client. It will also be necessary to conduct enhanced ongoing monitoring of the business relationship.

A PEP is an individual who is entrusted with prominent public functions, other than as a middle-ranking or more junior official (reg 35(12)). PEPs have been a focus for the Financial Action Task Force, EU members and other countries due to growing concerns about PEPs using their political positions to corruptly enrich themselves. Individuals with prominent public functions include the following:

(a) Heads of State, heads of government, ministers and deputy or assistant ministers;

(b) members of parliament;

(c) members of supreme courts, of constitutional courts or of other high-level judicial bodies whose decisions are not generally subject to further appeal, except in exceptional circumstances;

(d) members of courts of auditors or of the boards of central banks;

(e) ambassadors, chargés d'affaires and high-ranking officers in the armed forces;

(f) members of the administrative, management or supervisory bodies of State-owned enterprises.

Family members include a spouse, civil partner, children, their spouses or civil partners and parents. Known close associates include those with whom there are close business relationships.

Changes to the Regulations now mean that domestic PEPs (defined as individuals entrusted with prominent public functions by the UK), whilst still needing to be subject to enhanced due diligence, must be treated as a lower risk than overseas PEPs. The exception to this would be where there were enhanced risk factors present with the individual concerned, ie risk factors other than their position as a domestic PEP.

Where the solicitor is dealing with the PEP (and this includes where a PEP, family member or close associate is a beneficial owner of a client), additional obligations are placed on the solicitor, namely having approval of senior management (for example, the managing partner) to act for the client, taking adequate measures to establish the source of wealth and source of funds involved in the business relationship or proposed transactions, and conducting enhanced ongoing monitoring of the business relationship (reg 35(5)).

5.8.5 Ongoing monitoring

A solicitor is obliged to undertake ongoing monitoring of business relationships, to ensure that the transactions are consistent with the solicitor's knowledge of the client (reg 28(11)).

5.9 Training

Firms are obliged to provide (and maintain a record of) training to their employees in respect of money laundering (reg 24). Employees should be made aware of the law relating to money laundering, terrorist financing and to the requirements of data protection relating to them. The Regulations also specify that employees should be given regular training on how to recognise (and then deal with) transactions that potentially involve money laundering or terrorist financing.

The Regulations do not specify how the training should take place. However, the legal sector guidance suggests that appropriate methods of delivery may include face-to-face learning or e-learning. The guidance also recommends the use of a staff manual on money laundering issues.

Where no such training is given, this may provide the employee with a defence to some of the offences under the Proceeds of Crime Act 2002 (see **Chapter 6**).

5.10 Record keeping

A firm must keep various records in respect of money laundering. The records are a copy of any documents and information obtained by the solicitor to satisfy the due diligence requirements and sufficient supporting records (consisting of the original documents or copies) in respect of a transaction which is the subject of due diligence measures or ongoing monitoring to enable the transaction to be reconstructed (reg 40). These records must be kept for at least five years from when the business relationship ends or the end of the occasional transaction.

5.11 Economic crime

The Criminal Finances Act 2017 includes the corporate offence of failure to prevent the criminal facilitation of tax evasion. The Act applies to law firms as 'relevant bodies'.

The offence makes a firm liable for failing to prevent tax evasion offences by its employees or other 'associated persons'. Such offences include the fraudulent evasion of VAT, income tax, national insurance contributions and the common law offence of cheating the public revenue. There is strict liability for the offence in that no knowledge or intention is required on the part of the firm or its senior management. The only defence available is that the firm had in place reasonable prevention procedures or is able to show that it was reasonable not to have had such procedures in place. The penalty for breach is unlimited fines, and confiscation of assets may be ordered.

Firms should already have policies and procedures in place to comply with their obligations under the Regulations. However, firms will need to ensure that such policies and procedures also comply with the Criminal Finances Act 2017. For example, due diligence procedures will need to take into account specifically the risk of criminal facilitation of tax evasion posed by its partners and employees as well as by other 'associated persons' (ie agents of the firm or those who perform services for or on behalf of it, such as barristers, surveyors and foreign law firms) and be adapted or introduced accordingly. A firm-wide risk assessment, internal procedures, staff training and ongoing monitoring will also be required.

5.12 The UK financial sanctions regime

Under the legislation which makes up the UK financial sanctions regime, serious and extensive restrictions are placed on dealing with people or entities who are on the 'sanctions list' (designated persons) as a result of sanctions imposed by the UK, EU or United Nations. The regime applies to all law firms whether or not they are subject to the Regulations. There is a requirement to inform the Office of Financial Sanctions Implementation if it is known or reasonably suspected that a person is a designated person or has committed offences under financial sanctions and asset freezing regimes. If a firm wishes to act for such a person, and that person is not covered by a general OFSI licence, the firm must first obtain an individual licence to receive reasonable fees for the provision of legal advice. The sanctions list is public information and so discussing a person's sanctioned status does not amount to a tipping off offence (see **6.8**).

Under the provisions of the Economic Crime (Transparency and Enforcement) Act 2022, firms can now face liability for fines even where they have no knowledge or reasonable cause to suspect that a transaction to which they are a party is in breach of the sanctions regime.

Summary

- Money laundering is the process whereby the proceeds of crime are changed so that they appear to come from a legitimate source.

- The Government has introduced legislation to disrupt this process.

- Solicitors who undertake relevant business must comply with the Money Laundering, Terrorist Financing and Transfer of Funds (Information on the Payer) Regulations 2017 (SI 2017/692).

- Under the 2017 Regulations, firms must appoint a money laundering compliance officer and a nominated officer, who will receive internal reports concerning money laundering and must consider whether to report the matter to the NCA.

Sample questions

Question 1

A solicitor is instructed by a client in a family case. The client tells the solicitor that their marriage has broken down, and their spouse has already agreed to the family home and all other family assets being transferred to the client. The client instructs the solicitor to deal with the transfer of the assets in accordance with the agreement.

The client is known to the solicitor because they are both members of a local gym. The solicitor knows that the client has told others at the gym that their spouse is under criminal investigation for tax fraud.

Which of the following best explains the steps that the solicitor should take with regard to due diligence?

A   The solicitor should carry out enhanced due diligence because there is a high risk of money laundering.

B   The solicitor should carry out standard due diligence because the client has not personally been involved in any criminal activity.

C   The solicitor should carry out standard due diligence because the client is a private individual.

D   The solicitor should carry out simplified due diligence because family work presents a low risk of money laundering.

E   The solicitor does not need to carry out any due diligence because the client is already known to the solicitor.

Answer

Option A is correct. Due diligence is required irrespective of the fact that the solicitor has some personal knowledge of the client (option E therefore is wrong). Simplified due diligence is based on an assessment of the individual facts of the case, not on the type of work involved (option D is wrong). Options B and C do not represent the best answers because while normally standard due diligence would be appropriate, here the facts suggest a high risk of money laundering and so enhanced due diligence is required. The criminal investigation is relevant (even though the client is not the subject) and the willingness of the spouse to transfer all the assets to the client is unusual. The risk here is that the marriage breakdown is a sham and that the spouse is seeking to distance themselves from assets purchased with the proceeds of crime by transferring those assets to the complicit client.

Question 2

A solicitor is instructed by a client in the purchase of a property. At the first meeting, in accordance with the firm's client due diligence policy, the solicitor asks to see the client's passport. The client explains that they have just had to send the passport off for renewal and does not expect their new passport to arrive for several weeks. The client produces a bank statement showing the client's name and address and promises to bring in a photo card driving licence tomorrow.

The following day, the client says that they cannot find their driving licence. Instead the client produces a letter from the client's neighbour stating that they have known the client for two years and confirming the client's full name. The client then says that, as a demonstration of goodwill, the client will provide the solicitor with the full purchase price of the property in cash later that day.

Which of the following best explains what the solicitor should do?

A Proceed and complete the purchase because the bank statement contains the client's name and address.

B Refuse to act because the solicitor does not have sufficient verification of the client's identity.

C Agree to undertake the initial steps in the purchase pending receipt of the new passport because there is little risk of money laundering.

D Proceed and complete the purchase because the letter is independent verification of the client's identity.

E Agree to undertake the initial steps in the purchase pending speaking to the neighbour direct.

Answer

Option B is correct. As a general rule verification should be obtained at first contact. Verification must be obtained from a reliable source which is independent from the client. The letter would not fall within this description (meaning that option D is wrong), even if the contents are confirmed face to face (option E is wrong), as the neighbour is a personal friend and may have been duped by the client. Good practice dictates that verification should be based on at least one government document. A bank statement might be sufficient in combination with a government document, but not in isolation; accordingly, option A is not the best answer. It is possible to delay verification if, inter alia, there is little risk of money laundering. That cannot be the case here given the client's inability to produce suitable documentation and the cash payment proposal. The solicitor should refuse to act in these circumstances. Accordingly, option C is wrong.

6 Proceeds of Crime Act 2002

SQE1 syllabus

This chapter will enable you to achieve the SQE1 Assessment Specification in relation to Functioning Legal Knowledge concerned with Legal Services:

- The regulatory role of the Solicitors Regulation Authority.

- Overriding legal obligations.

- Purpose and scope of money laundering legislation including the international context.

- Circumstances encountered in the course of practice where suspicion of money laundering should be reported in accordance with the legislation.

- The appropriate person or body to whom suspicions should be reported, the approximate time for such reports to be made and the appropriate procedure to be followed.

- Direct involvement and non-direct involvement offences, and defences to those offences, under Proceeds of Crime Act 2002.

The offences under the Proceeds of Crime Act 2002 set out in this chapter may be referred to in the SQE1 assessment. Otherwise, references to cases and statutory or regulatory authorities in this chapter are provided for illustrative purposes only.

Learning outcomes

By the end of this chapter you will be able to apply relevant core legal principles and rules appropriately and effectively, at the level of a competent newly qualified solicitor in practice, to realistic client-based and ethical problems and situations in the following areas:

- The reporting of money laundering suspicions.
- The key offences under the Proceeds of Crime Act 2002.
- The defences to the key offences under the Proceeds of Crime Act 2002.

6.1 Introduction

The Proceeds of Crime Act 2002 is, like the Money Laundering Regulations (see **Chapter 5**), part of the UK's response to international efforts against money laundering.

The Proceeds of Crime Act 2002 is wide ranging and encompasses a variety of criminal behaviour. Of particular interest to the legal profession is that in addition to criminalising acts of money laundering itself, it creates a number of offences applicable to legitimate businesses, including solicitors, who fail to respond appropriately when faced with the money laundering activities of others.

Solicitors are often targeted by criminals seeking to launder their proceeds of crime or give their criminal activities the appearance of legitimacy (see **Chapter 5**). However, solicitors are at risk of committing criminal offences themselves if they are not vigilant as to the threat of money laundering and/or fail to report suspected money laundering to the appropriate authorities.

This chapter looks at:

- overview of offences
- s 328 Arranging
- s 329 Acquisition, use or possession
- s 327 Concealing etc
- s 330 Failure to disclose
- s 331 Failure to disclose (nominated officers)
- s 333A Tipping off
- s 342 Prejudicing an investigation
- Confidentiality
- Role of the SRA
- Warning signs

6.2 Overview of offences

The Proceeds of Crime Act 2002 (POCA 2002) creates three offences which involve the direct handling of the proceeds of crime. The offences are widely drafted. Whilst they encompass the actions of those who instigated the criminal behaviour in the first place, and their associates, they will also extend to the work carried out by solicitors where the effect of that work is to facilitate money laundering.

Under POCA 2002 it is an offence to:

* enter into, or become concerned in an arrangement, which a person knows or suspects facilitates the retention, use or control of the proceeds of crime (s 328);

* acquire, use or possess the proceeds of crime (s 329);

* conceal, disguise, convert or transfer the proceeds of crime, or remove the proceeds of crime from the jurisdiction of England and Wales (s 327).

In addition, POCA 2002 creates other offences targeted at the action or inaction of someone who becomes aware of possible money laundering. In the main these offences only apply to those in the regulated sector. This means that the offences will apply to most solicitors. The offences are:

* failure to disclose information about money laundering to the appropriate authorities (s 330);

* failure on the part of a firm's nominated officer to disclose information about money laundering to the appropriate authorities (s 331);

* 'tipping off' an individual that an investigation into money laundering is underway (s 333A);

* prejudicing an investigation into money laundering (s 342).

6.3 Section 328 Arranging

This is the offence involving direct involvement with the proceeds of crime which is most likely to be relevant to solicitors.

Section 328(1) Proceeds of Crime Act 2002 provides:

> A person commits an offence if he enters into or becomes concerned in an arrangement which he knows or suspects facilitates (by whatever means) the acquisition, retention, use or control of criminal property by or on behalf of another person.

Section 328 is widely drafted and encompasses virtually any act which assists in the process of money laundering by another person. There is not even a requirement that the funds actually pass through the hands of the person concerned with the arrangement, ie the solicitor.

Much of the mainstream work of solicitors could constitute an arrangement. For example, where a solicitor transfers a house to a relative of a client, the solicitor would '[become] concerned in an arrangement'.

6.3.1 'Know or suspect'

To constitute an offence under s 328, the individual must know or suspect that the arrangement facilitates some act regarding the proceeds of crime. The threshold for the mental element of the offence is therefore 'suspicion'. The test is a subjective one and the bar is set rather low:

R v Da Silva [2006] EWCA Crim 1654

This case was decided under earlier legislation, but the court made reference to the requirements under POCA 2002 which was in place by the time that the appeal hearing took place.

Lord Justice Longmore said:

> What then does the word 'suspecting' mean.....? It seems to us that the essential element in the word 'suspect' and its affiliates, in this context, is that the defendant must think that there is a possibility, which is more than fanciful, that the relevant facts exist. A vague feeling of unease would not suffice. But the statute does not require the suspicion to be 'clear' or 'firmly grounded and targeted on specific facts'...

It would therefore seem that all that is required for 'suspicion' is that there is a possibility, which is more than fanciful.

'Know or suspect' is a phrase which appears throughout the legislation.

6.3.2 Criminal property

A key element of the offence under s 328 (and other offences under POCA 2002) is that it concerns criminal property.

'Criminal property' is defined by s 340 as a person's direct or indirect benefit from criminal conduct. The definition includes not only, for example, the stolen property itself but also any profits made from the original crime.

To constitute 'criminal property' the person must know or suspect that the property constitutes or represents a benefit from criminal conduct.

There must have been an initial criminal offence committed for the property to become 'criminal'. 'Criminal conduct' is defined to include any offence committed within the United Kingdom, ranging from armed robbery to fraudulent receipt of welfare benefits.

The definition also includes an international element. The proceeds of criminal conduct committed abroad will come within the definition of criminal property if the conduct would have been criminal if it had occurred in the UK.

6.3.3 Litigation proceedings

In *Bowman v Fels* [2005] EWCA Civ 226, the Court of Appeal considered whether taking steps in litigation could be construed as 'arranging' under s 328. The Court concluded that taking steps in litigation (including pre-action steps) and the resolution of issues in a litigious context were excluded from the scope of s 328.

The current legal sector guidance provides that dividing assets in accordance with a court judgment (for example, following a divorce) also does not fall within the definition of arranging. However, the guidance goes on to state that careful consideration should be made of whether the client would be committing an offence by receiving stolen property. Being involved in the reinvestment of such assets would fall foul of s 328.

The solicitor would not be able to take advantage of this exclusion if the litigation was a sham created for the purposes of money laundering.

6.3.4 Authorised disclosure defence

6.3.4.1 Making an authorised disclosure

The making of an authorised disclosure is available as a defence to the offence under s 328 (and to the offences under s 329 and s 327 (see **6.4**.and **6.5**)). Authorised disclosures are dealt with under s 338.

Under s 338 the disclosure must be made by the person who, but for the disclosure, would be committing an offence. To be authorised under s 338, and therefore prevent an offence being committed, the disclosure must be in relation to criminal property and satisfy certain requirements as to its timing and the person to whom it must be made.

A disclosure is authorised under s 338 if it is made to a constable, an officer of His Majesty's Revenue and Customs or a nominated officer. Therefore, for solicitors in most cases it is the person appointed by the firm as the nominated officer to whom the disclosure should be made. The nominated officer is often referred to as the Money Laundering Reporting Officer (MLRO), although technically the two roles are distinct and may be fulfilled by different individuals within the firm.

It is the nominated officer's responsibility to report concerns about money laundering to the National Crime Agency (NCA). In the UK money laundering comes within the remit of the financial intelligence unit of the NCA. The NCA deals with law enforcement in the context of organised crime within the UK and works with foreign law enforcement agencies in respect of global organised crime.

A report made to the NCA by the nominated officer is called a suspicious activity report (SAR).

The NCA operates an online procedure for making suspicious activity reports. It is preferable for a report to be made online as this enables the report to be made at any time and actioned quickly. It is, however, possible to make a report by post using the NCA's standard forms.

The nominated officer is not under any obligation to make a SAR when concerns are raised by another person in the firm. It is for the nominated officer to exercise their own judgement in deciding whether the matter should be passed on to the NCA. Although the nominated officer risks committing a criminal offence if they fail to make a report where there were reasonable grounds to suspect money laundering (see **6.7**).

6.3.4.2 Disclosure prior to the act taking place

A solicitor does not commit an offence under s 328 if the solicitor makes an authorised disclosure to the firm's nominated officer as soon as is practically possible prior to the transaction taking place, and the consent of the nominated officer or the National Crime Agency (NCA) is obtained. This is a complete defence to a charge under s 328. However, it should be noted that the making of the authorised disclosure is not in itself sufficient. Proceeding without having obtained the appropriate consent remains an offence.

Once the nominated officer has made a suspicious activity report to the NCA, the nominated officer is unable to give consent until one of the following conditions is met:

(a) the nominated officer, having made a disclosure to the NCA, receives the consent of the NCA;

(b) the nominated officer, having made a disclosure to the NCA, hears nothing for seven working days (starting with the first working day after the disclosure is made);

(c) where consent is refused by the NCA, the nominated officer may not give consent unless consent is subsequently granted within 31 days starting on the day refusal is given, or a period of 31 days has expired from the date of refusal. This 31-day period gives the authorities time to take action to seize assets or take other action with respect to the money laundering. (The 31-day period can be extended in certain circumstances.)

Although the term used in the legislation is 'consent', a more accurate description (now adopted by the NCA) is 'a defence against money laundering'. The sole purpose and effect of consent is to provide a defence against a money laundering offence, it does not confirm that proceeding with the transaction is the right, ethical or even legal step to take. The solicitor must still look to the law, rules of professional conduct and wider considerations before deciding to proceed.

6.3.4.3 Disclosure during the prohibited act

A solicitor may seek to make an authorised disclosure whilst the prohibited act is ongoing. However, if the solicitor is to avoid breaching s 328 by making the disclosure, the solicitor must satisfy the provisions of s 338(2A):

(a) the disclosure is made whilst the prohibited act is ongoing; and

(b) when the solicitor began to do the act, the solicitor did not know or suspect that the property constituted or represented a person's benefit from criminal conduct; and

(c) the disclosure is made as soon as is practicable after the solicitor first knows or suspects that the property constitutes or represents a person's benefit from criminal conduct, and the disclosure is made on the solicitor's own initiative.

⭐ *Example*

A solicitor is conducting a conveyancing transaction on behalf of a client. Until the client exchanges contracts to sell the property, the solicitor has no knowledge or suspicion that the house was bought with the proceeds of crime. Accordingly, there is no breach of s 328, as the solicitor does not possess the requisite knowledge or suspicion. After contracts have been exchanged, the solicitor correctly begins to suspect that the house was bought with the proceeds of crime. Accordingly, the solicitor is now concerned in an arrangement which facilitates the acquisition, retention, use or control of criminal property and therefore is in breach of s 328.

In order to seek the protection of making an authorised disclosure, the solicitor must disclose their suspicions to the firm's nominated officer on the solicitor's own initiative and must do so as soon as is practicable after the first suspicions arise.

6.3.4.4 Disclosure after the prohibited act

A solicitor may also seek to make an authorised disclosure after the prohibited act has been completed. However, the solicitor must have a good reason for their failure to disclose prior to completing the act (s 338(3)). The disclosure must be made as soon as is practicable, and again the solicitor must make the disclosure on the solicitor's own initiative.

6.3.4.5 Reasonable excuse for non-disclosure

A solicitor may have a defence to breaching s 328 where the solicitor intended to make an authorised disclosure but has a reasonable excuse for failing to do so. 'Reasonable excuse' has not been defined by the courts, but it is likely to be narrowly construed, for example there may be a reasonable excuse where the relevant information is already in the public domain. Solicitors should certainly document their reasons for non-disclosure.

6.3.5 Overseas defence

There is a defence to s 328 where the individual knew or believed that the 'criminal conduct' occurred abroad and the conduct in question was lawful in the country where it took place. The Secretary of State has the power to override this provision.

6.3.6 Penalties

An individual convicted under s 328 may receive a maximum sentence of 14 years' imprisonment.

⭐ *Example*

Ayesha is a solicitor acting for a client on a corporate transaction. The client is buying Xan Ltd. During the course of due diligence Ayesha discovers that a number of Xan Ltd's lucrative contracts were obtained by paying bribes.

What should Ayesha do?

Ayesha needs to consider whether anything of a criminal nature has occurred. Obtaining property using bribes is a criminal offence. These contracts will have generated cash which will be owned by Xan Ltd. Therefore, when Ayesha's client buys the company, the client will be acquiring the proceeds of crime. Simply by completing the transaction Ayesha will be concerned in an arrangement which facilitates the acquisition, retention, use or control of criminal property, which is an offence under s 328 POCA 2002. Ayesha needs to report the matter to the firm's nominated officer. The nominated officer will then need to seek the consent of the NCA for the transaction to proceed.

6.4 Section 329 Acquisition, use or possession

A person commits an offence under s 329 POCA 2002 if they acquire, use or have possession of criminal property. 'Criminal property' has the same meaning as under s 328 (see **6.3.2**).

Typically, this provision will be used to prosecute those who had no involvement with the original crime, but have enjoyed the benefit (for example, family members who have lived off the proceeds of crime). However, it can be of relevance to solicitors. An issue may arise in connection with s 329 where, for example, a solicitor receives money for costs for work carried out for a client charged with a criminal offence and there is a possibility that the money in question is criminal property.

The authorised disclosure defence (see **6.3.4**) and the overseas defence (see **6.3.5**) also apply to s 329.

There is a further defence to s 329: the adequate consideration defence. An offence will not be committed if there was adequate consideration for acquiring, using and possessing the criminal property, unless the individual knew or suspected that those goods or services might help to carry out criminal conduct. The Crown Prosecution Service (CPS) guidance for prosecutors says that this defence applies where professional advisers, such as solicitors, receive money for or on account of costs, including disbursements. However, the fees charged must be reasonable and the defence is not available if the value of the work is significantly less than the money received.

An individual convicted under s 329 may receive a maximum sentence of 14 years' imprisonment.

6.5 Section 327 Concealing etc

It is an offence under s 327 to conceal, disguise, convert or transfer criminal property or remove it from England Wales Scotland or Northern Ireland. 'Criminal property' has the same meaning as under s 328 (see **6.3.2**).

This is the main money laundering offence. There is the potential for solicitors to fall foul of this provision because the purpose of many transactions conducted by solicitors is to 'convert' (for example, money into property) or to 'transfer' (for example, money or ownership between parties).

The authorised disclosure defence (see **6.3.4**) and the overseas defence (see **6.3.5**) also apply to s 327.

6.6 Section 330 Failure to disclose

The purpose behind this offence is to ensure that information about suspected money laundering is passed to the authorities promptly so that a proper investigation can be carried out.

A person commits an offence under s 330 POCA 2002 if:

(a) he knows or suspects, or has reasonable grounds to know or suspect, that a person is engaged in money laundering;

(b) the information comes to him in the course of a business in the regulated sector;

(c) the information may assist in identifying the money launderer or the location of any laundered property; and

(d) he does not make a disclosure as soon as is practicable.

It should be noted that it is not necessary for money laundering to have actually occurred for the offence to be committed. The CPS guidance makes clear that a prosecution will be pursued even in circumstances where there is insufficient evidence to prove that money laundering was planned or had taken place.

6.6.1 Objective test

The wording of this offence incorporates the 'know or suspect' test. However, in s 330 there is the addition of the wording 'or has reasonable grounds to know or suspect'. This means that a solicitor will commit this offence even where the solicitor genuinely did not know or suspect that a person was engaged in money laundering. The court will consider, based on the information available to the solicitor at the time, whether the solicitor *should* have known (or at least suspected) that money laundering was occurring. Accordingly, turning a blind eye to a transaction will not provide the solicitor with a defence.

The justification for the objective test is that those working in the regulated sector are expected to maintain greater vigilance and employ higher standards of care.

6.6.2 Regulated sector

Firms will be within the 'regulated sector' if they undertake relevant business (POCA 2002, Sch 9) and this extends to those providing legal services. Most firms of solicitors will fall within the regulated sector for at least some of the work which they carry out. The definition of 'regulated sector' is closely aligned to the definition given in the Money Laundering Regulations (see **Chapter 5**).

6.6.3 The information

The information obtained by the solicitor must be of some use to the authorities. Accordingly, the solicitor must be able to identify, or believe the information may assist in identifying:

(a) the money launderer; or

(b) the location of the laundered property.

If the solicitor is genuinely unable to provide this information, the solicitor will not breach s 330.

The solicitor cannot blindly assume that the information will be of no use to the authorities. When considering whether the solicitor has breached s 330, the court will consider whether it would have been reasonable to expect the solicitor to believe that the information would assist in identifying the offender or locating the laundered property.

6.6.4 Disclosure

A failure to make the required disclosure is part of the offence. To meet the requirements of s 330 the disclosure must be made to the firm's nominated officer or the NCA as soon as practically possible. The disclosure must comprise the reasons behind the solicitor's knowledge or suspicions of money laundering and, as far as is possible, the identity of the money launderer and the whereabouts of the laundered property. If the disclosure is made, the solicitor will not commit the s 330 offence.

A solicitor will not commit this offence where the solicitor intended to make a disclosure but has a reasonable excuse for not doing so. There is no guidance on what would constitute a reasonable excuse; however, the courts are likely to take a stringent view.

6.6.5 Training defence

A further defence under s 330 concerns the training provided to an individual. Firms undertaking 'relevant business' are obliged to provide anti-money laundering training to their employees. The employee will not commit an offence if they do not know or suspect that a client is engaged in money laundering, but there were reasonable grounds to suspect that the client was engaged in money laundering, and the employee has not received proper training.

6.6.6 Legal professional privilege defence

A solicitor is under a duty at common law to keep confidential certain information given to them from a client. This is referred to as legal professional privilege. Communications will be protected from disclosure if they fall within 'advice privilege' or 'litigation privilege'. Advice privilege applies to communications between a solicitor, acting in that capacity, and a client, if they are both confidential and for the purpose of seeking legal advice from a legal professional or providing it to a client. Litigation privilege protects confidential communications made after litigation has started, or is reasonably in prospect, between a solicitor and client or solicitor and third party for the sole or dominant purpose of litigation. However, legal professional privilege cannot be relied upon where the communication takes place with the purpose of carrying out an offence.

POCA 2002 mirrors the common law position, in that a solicitor is not obliged under s 330 to disclose any information that comes to the solicitor as a professional legal adviser in privileged circumstances, eg in connection with giving or seeking legal advice, or in relation to legal proceedings, whether contemplated or actual. However, this exemption does not apply where the information is communicated with the intention of furthering a criminal purpose (eg money laundering).

6.6.7 Overseas defence

A solicitor will not breach s 330 for failing to disclose where the solicitor believes that the money laundering is taking place outside of the UK, and money laundering is not unlawful in that country. The Secretary of State has the power to override this defence, but at the time of writing has not taken any steps to do so.

6.6.8 Penalties

A person convicted of an offence under s 330 may receive a maximum sentence of five years' imprisonment.

6.7 Section 331 Failure to disclose (nominated officers)

Under s 331 a nominated officer will commit an offence if they know or suspect, or have reasonable grounds to know or suspect, money laundering, as a consequence of their role as person nominated to receive disclosures under s 330, and fail to make the necessary disclosure to the NCA as soon as practical.

The nominated officer will have a defence if they have a reasonable excuse for not disclosing the information.

6.8 Section 333A Tipping off

'Tipping off' refers to alerting someone suspected of money laundering (or an associate) to the fact that an investigation has started or is anticipated.

6.8.1 The offences

There are two aspects of tipping off that must be avoided under s 333A.

Both offences are intended to ensure that information is not leaked to the money launderer or another third party before the authorities have had the opportunity to investigate the matter and consider whether any enforcement action is necessary.

Under both offences there is no requirement to show that the tipping off was intended to alert the money launderer or intended to prejudice any investigation.

6.8.1.1   Disclosing a disclosure

Rather tortuously it is an offence under s 333A(1) to disclose to any person that a relevant disclosure (on money laundering) has been made if that disclosure is likely to prejudice any investigation that follows such a report. The information on which the disclosure is made must have come to the person in the course of a business in the regulated sector.

A relevant disclosure includes one made to the firm's nominated officer or the NCA. For example, this offence would apply where a solicitor informs their client that an authorised disclosure (see **6.3.4**) has been made, with the intention of the client taking steps to frustrate any action taken by the law enforcement authorities.

⭐ *Example*

*Wilkie instructs his solicitor to sell his house. The solicitor suspects that the house was purchased with the proceeds of tax evasion and so makes an authorised disclosure to the firm's nominated officer. The transaction cannot proceed at least until the solicitor obtains the consent of the firm's nominated officer or the NCA (see **6.3.4.2**). Wilkie demands to know why his house sale is not making progress. A junior member of staff receives Wilkie's call and, having checked the file, informs Wilkie that the delay is due to an authorised disclosure having been made. In these circumstances the member of staff may breach s 333A unless they can rely on one of the defences (see **6.8.2**).*

6.8.1.2   Disclosing an investigation

Section 333A(3) contains a more general offence. The offence is committed where a disclosure is made to any person that an investigation into allegations that an offence under POCA 2002 has been committed is being carried out, or is being contemplated, and that disclosure is likely to prejudice the money laundering investigation. Again, the information on which the disclosure is made must have come to the person in the course of a business in the regulated sector.

6.8.2   Defences

It is a defence under s 333A if the person who made the disclosure did not know or suspect that the disclosure would prejudice an investigation into money laundering (s 333D(3) and (4)). The ambit of this defence is unclear. It may cover the situation where, for example, a solicitor informs a client about an investigation believing that the client will fully cooperate with the authorities.

It is a defence under s 333A if the disclosure is made by an adviser to their client for the purposes of dissuading the client from engaging in the alleged money laundering (333D(2)), although this exception should be treated with caution.

6.8.3   Penalties

Both tipping off offences carry a maximum penalty of an unlimited fine, and/or a maximum prison sentence of two years.

6.9   Prejudicing an investigation

Under s 342 a person will commit an offence if they know or suspect that a money laundering investigation has or is about to be commenced and they make a material disclosure to any other person which is likely to prejudice the investigation or interferes with relevant material. This is similar to the tipping off offence but extends to non-regulated individuals.

6.10 Confidentiality

It will be evident from the above that POCA 2002 often requires a solicitor to provide information about their clients in order avoid committing an offence. However, as a matter of professional conduct a solicitor owes a client the duty of confidentiality.

Under Paragraph 6.3 SRA Code of Conduct for Solicitors, RELs and RFLs a solicitor is required to keep confidential the affairs of clients (including former clients) unless disclosure is required or permitted by law or the client consents. When making a disclosure under s 338, the legislation expressly provides that such a disclosure will not breach this duty and so is required/permitted by law. Nevertheless a solicitor should be mindful of the importance of the duty of confidentiality, and seek advice when uncertain as to whether to report confidential information.

6.11 The role of the SRA

The SRA has a supervisory role under the legislation. Indeed, the SRA regards anti-money laundering to be one of the most important aspects of its function.

However, the SRA also has a regulatory function. A solicitor who is shown to have a direct involvement in money laundering will be in breach of SRA Principle 4 which requires solicitors to act with honesty. Similarly, the commission of any of the other offences is likely to breach SRA Principle 1 (the duty to uphold the rule of law and the administration of justice).

Consequently, a solicitor who falls foul of the POCA 2002 is also likely to face disciplinary proceedings and, given the nature of the misconduct, significant sanctions.

6.12 Warning signs

A solicitor can become caught up in money laundering in a number of ways. At one end of the spectrum there will be a very small number of solicitors who are knowingly and deliberately complicit in the criminal activity. At the other end of the spectrum are those who have been completely duped and for whom no amount of vigilance could have prevented their involvement. But in between are the majority who need to be alert to the warning signs or 'red flags', ask appropriate questions and keep their relationship with their clients under constant review in order to avoid becoming unwittingly or carelessly involved.

It goes without saying that the SRA expects solicitors and firms to comply with all money laundering legislation. However, the SRA also requires solicitors and firms to be able to spot the warning signs or indicators of money laundering and to act appropriately, for example by reporting the matter to the firm's nominated officer or the NCA. The SRA includes a number of indicators in its Warning Notice: Money Laundering and Terrorist Financing:

(a) The client

A number of aspects of the personality or nature of the client may be indicators. For example, the client who is secretive, obstructive or evasive, avoids personal contact, refuses to provide information or documentation or has criminal associations.

(b) Funding

Where the solicitor is carrying out some form of transaction for the client, an unusual source of funding may be an indicator. For example, large cash payment, unexplained payments from a third party, loans from non-institutional lenders or the use of multiple accounts or foreign accounts.

(c) The transaction

A transaction with unusual features may be an indicator. For example, the transaction is loss making, repetitive instructions, unexplained urgency, there is no obvious commercial purpose, or litigation which is settled too easily or quickly.

(d) Unusual instructions

Indicators here may be instructions which are unusual for the firm's business. For example, instructions which are outside the solicitor's/firm's area of expertise or normal business, the client is not local to the firm and there is no explanation as to why the firm has been chosen, the client is willing to pay high fees, or the client appears unconcerned about the transaction.

(e) Geographical concerns

For example, the unexplained movement of monies between other jurisdictions or connections with suspect jurisdictions.

Summary

The key offences under the Proceeds of Crime Act 2002 are:

- Entering into, or becoming concerned in, an arrangement which a person knows or suspects facilitates the retention, use or control of the proceeds of crime (s 328).

- Acquiring, using or possessing the proceeds of crime (s 329).

- Concealing, disguising, converting or transferring the proceeds of crime, or removing the proceeds of crime from the jurisdiction of England and Wales (s 327).

- Failing to disclose information about money laundering to the appropriate authorities (s 330).

- Failure on the part of a firm's nominated officer to disclose information about money laundering to the appropriate authorities (s 331).

- 'Tipping off' an individual that an investigation into money laundering is underway (s 333A).

- Prejudicing an investigation into money laundering (s 342).

Sample questions

Question 1

A solicitor is instructed on the purchase of company shares. The solicitor discovers that a colleague in the firm has been instructed by the same client in respect of an investigation by the French tax authorities into certain of the client's business activities in France which are alleged to amount to tax fraud. The solicitor makes an authorised disclosure to the firm's nominated officer. The nominated officer does not go on to make a suspicious activity report to the National Crime Agency. Forty-eight hours later, having heard nothing from the nominated officer, the solicitor buys the shares on the client's behalf.

Is the solicitor likely to have committed the offence of 'arranging' under s 328 Proceeds of Crime Act 2002?

A Yes, because a suspicious activity report has not been made to the National Crime Agency.

B Yes, because the solicitor did not have appropriate consent to proceed with the purchase of the shares.

C No, because the solicitor made an authorised disclosure to the firm's nominated officer.

D No, because the client has not yet been convicted of any criminal offence.

E No, because any criminal conduct took place outside the UK.

Answer

Option B is the best answer. An authorised disclosure was required to prevent falling foul of s 328 despite the fact that the alleged criminal activity took place outside the UK (fraud is a criminal offence in France) and despite the lack of a conviction (suspicion is all that is required). However, the making of an authorised disclosure is not a sufficient defence in itself. Having made the disclosure the solicitor will still have committed the offence by proceeding with the purchase without consent. The duty to make a suspicious activity report lies with the nominated officer and a failure to make the report has no relevance to the solicitor's liability under s 328.

Question 2

A junior solicitor, who works for a firm in Newcastle, is instructed on the purchase of a residential property by a client who lives in Southampton. The client provides the solicitor with the purchase price of the property in cash. The client then pulls out of the purchase and asks the solicitor to return the purchase money to the client by cheque.

Which of the following best describes how the solicitor should respond?

A Inform their head of department about the client's request.

B Do nothing.

C Tell the firm's nominated officer that there is a suspicion of money laundering.

D Make a full file note of the client's request.

E Send the cheque.

Answer

Option C is correct. There are reasonable grounds for suspecting that the client is engaged in money laundering (geographical distance between solicitor and client and the use of cash). The solicitor will commit the failure to disclose offence under s 330 if they do not make a relevant disclosure. The solicitor should therefore inform the firm's nominated officer giving details of their suspicions. Option B is wrong as doing nothing is not an option in this case. Neither option A nor D is the best answer because, while making a file note and informing the head of department are good ideas they will not save the solicitor from committing the offence. Finally, option E is wrong. By sending the cheque the solicitor is likely to commit other offences (eg arranging under s 328).

Question 3

A partner in a firm is acting for a client in the purchase of a business. The firm receives a telephone call from the client's wife. The partner, who is in a meeting, asks a junior solicitor to take the call. In doing so the partner says that the client has given permission for any information about the purchase to be discussed with his wife.

The solicitor takes the call. The client's wife asks for an update on the progress of the purchase. On checking the file, the solicitor tells the client's wife that the client provided the money for the purchase in cash and the partner has concerns that the client may have obtained some of the money as a result of tax fraud and that consequently the purchase is on hold whilst the firm considers making a suspicious activity report to the National Crime Agency.

Which of the following best explains whether the solicitor has committed a 'tipping off' offence under s 333A Proceeds of Crime Act 2002?

A An offence has not been committed because the disclosure was authorised by the partner.

B An offence has not been committed because the solicitor did not intend to prejudice an investigation.

C An offence has not been committed because the disclosure was not made to the client.

D An offence has been committed because there is strong evidence that the client has been engaged in money laundering.

E An offence has been committed because the disclosure is likely to prejudice any investigation into money laundering.

Answer

Option E is correct. A key element of the offence is that the disclosure is likely to prejudice an investigation. Making the disclosure to the client's wife is highly likely to prejudice the investigation. However, the solicitor does not need to have intended this outcome (option B therefore is wrong). A tipping off offence under s 333A(3) does not depend on the strength of evidence of money laundering (option D is wrong); even the contemplation of an investigation is sufficient. Tipping off offences can be committed where a disclosure is made to any person, meaning that option C is wrong. Finally, option A is wrong as there is no scope for the tipping off to be authorised, and in any event the partner authorised the conversation taking place, not its content.

7 Funding Options

SQE1 syllabus

This chapter will enable you to achieve the SQE1 Assessment Specification in relation to Functioning Legal Knowledge concerned with Legal Services:

- Funding options for legal services.
- Private funding.
- Conditional fee arrangements.
- Damages-based agreements.
- Fixed fees.
- Third party funding.
- Legal expenses insurance.

Note that for SQE1, candidates are not usually required to recall specific case names or cite statutory or regulatory authorities. Cases are provided for illustrative purposes only.

Learning outcomes

By the end of this chapter you will be able to apply relevant core legal principles and rules appropriately and effectively, at the level of a competent newly qualified solicitor in practice, to realistic client-based and ethical problems and situations in the following areas:

- Professional conduct considerations in relation to funding.
- Types of funding.
- Availability of funding options.

7.1 Introduction

For any client one of the most important aspects of legal services is the question of how they will be paid for. The costs involved in the case and how to finance them will be at the forefront of the client's mind and the issue must be addressed at the earliest opportunity.

For some clients the question will be, 'can I afford to pay?'; for others the question will be, 'can I afford not to?'. When, perhaps, liberty, reputation or a child's future is at stake, the importance of the matter to the client may outweigh the monetary cost. In past years those who needed access to justice, but could not afford to pay for a solicitor, could turn to public funding to have their costs paid (see **Chapter 8**). However, whilst this still remains an option for some, the ambit of public funding is now severely restricted.

In recent years pragmatism has required law firms to open up to a variety of methods of paying for legal services. A solicitor must understand the funding options available in order to be able to play their part in agreeing upon the method which both addresses the client's requirements and meets the business needs of the firm.

This chapter looks at:

- the retainer
- professional conduct
- private funding
- fixed fees
- contentious and non-contentious business
- funding civil litigation

7.2 The retainer

The retainer is the contractual relationship which exists between solicitor and client. One important aspect of the contract which must be agreed at the outset is the fees and charges the solicitor will levy for acting for the client and the manner in which those fees and charges will be met.

Although, as in any contractual relationship, the parties are generally free to agree terms, certain restrictions are placed upon the fees a solicitor may charge, and also upon how the solicitor will be remunerated, by the Solicitors Regulation Authority (SRA) and the general law. These restrictions vary depending upon what type of work the solicitor has agreed to carry out for the client.

This chapter deals with the funding options available to clients. For a discussion of fees, bills and challenging a solicitor's charges (see **Ethics and Professional Conduct**).

7.3 Professional conduct

A solicitor may charge a client for work done on a number of different bases. Whichever method of charging the client and solicitor agree, the solicitor must always comply with their overarching professional conduct obligations.

Paragraph 8.7 of the SRA Code of Conduct for Solicitors, RELs and RFLs provides that a solicitor must provide clients with the best possible information about how their matter will be priced and, both at the time of engagement and when appropriate as their matter progresses, about the likely overall cost of a matter and any costs incurred. The term 'costs' is defined in the SRA Glossary as meaning the solicitor's fees and disbursements.

In addition, the SRA Transparency Rules (see **Ethics and Professional Conduct**) require that, in relation to certain types of legal services, particular costs information must be provided. That information includes the circumstances in which clients may have to make any payments themselves for the services provided by the solicitor, including from any damages received.

The rules of professional conduct are not solely concerned with costs information; they also extend to the level of charges. A solicitor must act in the best interests of the client (SRA Principle 7) and act with integrity (SRA Principle 5). Excessive charges for work done could breach both these Principles. Similarly, excessive charges may breach Paragraph 1.2 of the SRA Code of Conduct for Solicitors, RELs and RFLs which provides that a solicitor must not abuse their position by taking unfair advantage of the client. That said, it is inevitable that firms will have regard to their own interests when negotiating the terms of the retainer. A prospective client cannot expect a solicitor to act solely in the client's interests when agreeing the level of remuneration.

Ultimately, of course, the client has the right to challenge a solicitor's bill. In most cases this may involve asking the court to assess the costs. The court will reduce the bill if the amount charged is unreasonable. This is an obvious restraint on the amount that a solicitor can charge. Where a costs officer (when assessing a solicitor's bill in a non-contentious matter) reduces the amount of the costs by more than 50%, they must inform the Solicitors Regulation Authority. (See **Ethics and Professional Conduct**.)

A range of funding options is discussed below. Under the SRA Code of Conduct for Solicitors, RELs and RFLs there is no obligation to offer alternative funding options or to agree to act for a client under any of them. However, a solicitor should make the client aware of the funding options and, if necessary, direct the client to take separate advice on their availability. For example, a solicitor may not carry out legal aid work (see **Chapter 8**), but if the solicitor thinks that the client may be eligible the solicitor must advise the client accordingly and, if necessary, direct the client elsewhere.

Paragraph 3.4 of the SRA Code of Conduct for Solicitors, RELs and RFLs requires a solicitor to consider and take into account the client's attributes, needs and circumstances. This requirement will apply when selecting and agreeing the appropriate funding option for the client's case.

7.4 Private funding

A client may choose to fund their solicitor's fees privately or simply have no other alternative. This is the traditional method of funding and it remains appropriate for many clients.

The solicitor's fees are calculated according to the time spent on the case at a given hourly charging rate (disbursements and expenses are charged separately). The client will be informed at the start of the matter which fee earners will be working on the client's file, and the fee earners' respective charge-out rates. The ultimate cost to the client is open-ended because it will depend on how long it takes to conclude the case and how much work the solicitor has to undertake on the client's behalf. Nevertheless, the solicitor must still give the client the best possible information on the likely overall cost of a matter (see **7.3**).

With this type of funding the client is personally responsible for solicitor's fees and disbursements irrespective of the outcome of the case.

7.5 Fixed fees

A solicitor may agree with the client to complete the work for a fixed fee, or for a fixed fee plus VAT and disbursements. In a sense this is a type of private funding because the client is, again, personally responsible for paying the solicitor's charges, but with a fixed fee the amount to be charged is established and known at the outset.

Fixed fees are common in some types of work, such as conveyancing transactions. However, particularly given the restrictions on the availability of legal aid in civil cases (see **Chapter 8**), it is not unusual nowadays for a client to conduct the case themselves, only instructing a solicitor to carry out a specific step in the proceedings, such as drafting a document or attending a hearing, often on a fixed fee basis.

It is vital that the solicitor obtains all the relevant information in order to set a fixed fee at a reasonable but remunerative level. A fixed fee cannot be altered at a later date (unless the client agrees) if the work turns out to be more expensive than the solicitor first expected.

Inventors Friend Ltd v Leathes Prior (a firm) [2011] EWHC 711 (QB)

A firm of solicitors agreed a fixed fee to briefly review and comment on the terms of a document. The fee was agreed before the solicitor involved had seen the actual document. The client later sued the firm for negligence.

Cranston J commented: 'When solicitors undertake work at a specific fee, they are generally speaking obliged to complete it exercising the ordinary standard of care, even if it has become unremunerative.'

7.6 Contentious and non-contentious business

The Solicitors Act 1974 permits solicitors to enter into two particular types of arrangements with their clients which impact on remuneration. These are termed contentious and non-contentious business agreements.

Contentious business is defined as 'business done, whether as a solicitor or an advocate, in or for the purposes of proceedings begun before a court or an arbitrator, not being business which falls within the definition of non-contentious business or common form probate business' (s 87 Solicitors Act 1974). Accordingly, contentious business is work done in relation to proceedings. However, contentious business starts only once proceedings have been issued.

Somewhat unhelpfully, non-contentious business is defined as 'any business done as a solicitor which is not contentious business' (s 87 Solicitors Act 1974). This includes obvious examples such as conveyancing or commercial drafting work.

7.6.1 Non-contentious business agreements

A solicitor and client may enter into a non-contentious business agreement in respect of the solicitor's remuneration for any non-contentious work. Under this agreement the solicitor may be remunerated by a gross sum, an hourly rate, commission, a percentage, a salary or otherwise.

To be enforceable, the agreement must comply with s 57 Solicitors Act 1974. For example, the agreement must:

(a) be in writing;

(b) be signed by the client;

(c) contain all the terms of the agreement (including whether disbursements and VAT are included in the agreed remuneration).

Where the relevant provisions have been complied with, the client will be unable to apply to have the bill assessed by the court. However, the court may set the agreement aside or reduce remuneration if the amount charged by the solicitor is unfair or unreasonable.

7.6.2 Contentious business agreements

A solicitor may enter into a contentious business agreement in respect of their remuneration for contentious work completed on behalf of the client (ss 59–63 Solicitors Act 1974).

The agreement may provide for the solicitor to be remunerated by reference to a gross sum, an hourly rate, a salary or otherwise.

In order to be enforceable, the agreement must comply with certain requirements, including:

(a) the agreement must state it is a contentious business agreement;

(b) the agreement must be in writing;

(c) the agreement must be signed by the client; and

(d) the agreement must contain all the terms.

Where the contentious business agreement is enforceable, the client will be unable to apply to court for an assessment of costs (except where the agreement provides that the solicitor is to be remunerated by reference to an hourly rate). However, the court may set aside the agreement or reduce remuneration if it is unfair or unreasonable.

A contentious business agreement does not, of itself, give the solicitor a cause of action against the client for their costs. The solicitor cannot simply sue on an unpaid bill. Instead, a solicitor seeking to enforce the agreement must first seek permission from the court to do so. If the court determines the agreement to be fair and reasonable, it will enforce it; if not, the court will set aside the agreement (and assess the costs as if the agreement had never been made).

7.6.3 Criticism of the legislation

The categorisation of business as either contentious or non-contentious under the Solicitors Act 1974 in essence hangs on whether or not proceedings have been issued. The categorisation is important. For example, s 74(3) limits the fees that can be charged in certain circumstances, but this is only applicable to 'contentious' business. The categorisation has been criticised by members of the judiciary and others as being artificial and out of step with modern practices. For example, somewhat illogically resolving claims via online pre-action portals (such as that for road traffic claims) constitutes non-contentious business under the Act. In *Belsner v CAM Legal Services Ltd* [2022] EWCA Civ 1387, Sir Geoffrey Vos MR commented, 'I have no doubt that [the Solicitors Act 1974] is in urgent need of legislative attention.'

7.7 Funding civil litigation

It is entirely possible for a client in a civil litigation case to agree to pay their solicitor's fees on, say, the basis of a traditional hourly charging rate irrespective of the outcome of the case. However, the nature of civil litigation is such that there are a number of other funding options open to the client.

7.7.1 Solicitor and client costs and costs between the parties

In litigation the distinction must be drawn between solicitor and client costs (ie the fees that the client has agreed to pay to their own solicitor) and costs that may be awarded between the parties at the end of the case. A solicitor must explain this distinction to the client at the outset of the case.

If the client loses the case, the client will usually have to pay their own solicitor's costs and, in addition, their opponent's costs. The general rule is that the unsuccessful party will be ordered to pay the costs of the successful party. The amount to be paid will be agreed, fixed or assessed by the court.

If the client wins the case, the client will still be responsible for their own solicitor's costs. Usually the opponent will be ordered to pay costs. Again, this will be an agreed amount or a sum assessed by the court or the amount determined by the fixed recoverable costs regime. If the costs recovered are, as is usual, less than the costs paid, the client will have to bear the loss. Similarly, the client may recover no costs at all (for example, because the opponent is bankrupt) in which case the client will have to pay their own solicitor's costs in full.

7.7.2 Variable fees

A solicitor is permitted, in certain circumstances, to charge a fee which varies according to the outcome of the matter.

For many years, fees dependant on the outcome of the case were outlawed because it was feared that they would compromise the solicitor's impartiality and create a conflict between solicitor and client. However, eventually this view was relaxed and now such fees are permitted in limited situations. Two types of fees arrangements are permitted, namely conditional fee agreements and damages-based agreements.

7.7.2.1 Conditional fee agreements

A conditional fee agreement (CFA) is defined by s 58(2)(a) Courts and Legal Services Act 1990 as:

> an agreement with a person providing advocacy or litigation services which provides for his fees and expenses, or any part of them, to be payable only in specified circumstances.

The 'specified circumstances' are whether or not the client succeeds with a claim or, alternatively, successfully defends a claim.

Although often referred to as a 'no win, no fee' agreement, the essence of a CFA is that the client pays a different amount for the legal services received depending on the outcome of the case. Under a CFA the solicitor receives no payment, or less than normal payment, if the case is lost, but receives normal, or higher than normal, payment if the client is successful.

The usual justification for CFAs is that they provide access to justice for those for whom it would otherwise be denied. However, there is no requirement that the client must be unable to fund the case by other means.

If a claim is successful, the solicitor will receive an enhanced fee to reflect that success. The higher fee payable (the success fee) must be expressed as a percentage increase of the fee that would be payable if there was no CFA. Normally the fee payable is based on the solicitor's usual hourly charging rates. For example, if a solicitor would normally charge £200 an hour, a 10% success fee would mean an additional £20 per hour. The fee is not based on the solicitor receiving any proportion of money recovered by the client.

From the solicitor's point of view it is essential that the CFA complies with all formal requirements. If the CFA is judged to be invalid, the solicitor will not be able to recover any fees under it. A CFA is enforceable only if it meets the requirements of ss 58 and 58A Courts and Legal Services Act 1990. These provide that a CFA:

(a) may be entered into in relation to any civil litigation matter, except family proceedings;

(b) must be in writing; and

(c) must state the percentage by which the amount of the fee that would be payable if it were not a CFA is to be increased.

The success fee cannot exceed 100% of the solicitor's normal charges. In personal injury cases there is an additional cap of 25% of the general damages recovered.

If the client wins the case and the opponent is ordered to pay the client's costs, these cannot include the success fee. That will be payable by the client.

Under the wording of the legislation it is possible for disbursements to be included as part of the agreement. However, most firms exclude disbursements simply because they do not want to run the risk of being left out of pocket. Therefore if the client loses the case, whilst they will not usually have to pay their own solicitor's fees, they will be liable for disbursements, such as counsel's fees or the costs of an expert witness. In addition the client will also be ordered to pay the opponent's costs, including disbursements. The client may not be in a position to pay these disbursements and/or may be concerned by the fact that they will not know until the end of the litigation whether they are liable to their opponent for costs and, if so, for how much.

⭐ **Example**

Imran is a solicitor. Imran is approached by Selina in relation to a contract dispute. Imran agrees to take on the case under a conditional fee agreement. Imran's usual charging rate is £200 per hour. Imran proposes a 'no win, no fee' conditional fee agreement with a success fee of 40%. This means that Imran's hourly charge out rate will be £280 per hour if Selina wins her claim. Selina agrees.

Scenario 1

The judge finds in Selina's favour and she is awarded damages of £20,000. Imran's bill totals £3,000 but the success fee increases this to £4,200. The 'usual' fees of £3,000 and any disbursements would be recoverable from Selina's opponent but Selina is responsible for any shortfall and also the success fee of £1,200, which would be paid from her damages.

Scenario 2

Selina loses the case and she is ordered to pay her opponent's costs and disbursements. In addition, Selina must pay her own solicitor's disbursements but she is not liable for the bill of £3,000 (nor the success fee).

Faced with the prospect of having to pay their own disbursements and their opponent's costs, a client may benefit from purchasing after-the-event insurance (ATE) (see **7.7.3.2**). This type of legal expenses insurance policy provides cover for the other side's costs and the client's own disbursements in the event of losing the case.

Whilst ATE insurance will cover the client's disbursements in the event that the client loses, in practice the client will be paying for those disbursements on an ongoing basis during the course of the litigation. To assist in these circumstances some banks and many ATE insurers offer loans to fund disbursements. Counsel may be willing to enter into a CFA with the solicitor (or sometimes with the client) in respect of their fees. However, such an arrangement cannot be entered into with an expert witness, because an expert's evidence must be impartial and therefore should not be capable of being influenced by the outcome of the case.

In entering into a CFA, a solicitor takes a financial risk. A solicitor should always conduct a risk assessment before entering into a CFA taking account of such factors as:

(a) the chances of the client succeeding on liability;

(b) the likely amount of the damages;

(c) the length of time it will take for the case to reach trial;

(d) the number of hours the solicitor is likely to have to spend on the case.

The risk assessment should also inform the success fee. It should not be set arbitrarily or automatically set at the highest level. The solicitor should advise the client on how the risk assessment is reflected in the success fee or, at the very least, be able to demonstrate that they gave very clear advice on how the success fee was arrived at.

Herbert v HH Law Ltd [2019] EWCA Civ 527

In this case it was held that a client could not be said to have given informed consent to a 100% success fee applied as standard without any account being taken of the individual risks in the client's case.

Sir Terence Etherton MR commented 'in the context of a conditional fee agreement, the amount of a success fee is traditionally related to litigation risk, as reasonably perceived by the solicitor or counsel at the time the agreement was made. Across the broad range of litigation, it would be unusual for it not to be.'

CFAs have become increasingly popular, partly filling the void created by the removal of legal aid for most civil cases. A CFA provides the client with the security of knowing that they will not receive a large bill from their solicitor at the end of the case. For the solicitor there is the opportunity to receive higher fees, but there is also the risk of receiving nothing at all if the case is lost.

7.7.2.2 Damages-based agreements

A damages-based agreement (DBA) is an agreement in which the solicitor agrees to receive payment for their services only if the client is successful in their claim; and the amount of the solicitor's fee is linked to the level of compensation/damages obtained.

A DBA is defined by s 58AA(3)(a) Courts and Legal Services Act 1990 as:

> an agreement between a person providing advocacy services, litigation services or claims management services and the recipient of those services which provides that—

> (i) the recipient is to make a payment to the person providing the services if the recipient obtains a specified financial benefit in connection with the matter in relation to which the services are provided, and

> (ii) the amount of that payment is to be determined by reference to the amount of the financial benefit obtained.

Therefore under a DBA if the client receives a financial benefit (usually in the form of damages paid by the opponent) the solicitor's fee is an agreed percentage of the compensation received. For example, if the client recovers £100,000 and the DBA is set at 10% then the client pays the solicitor a fee of £10,000. This is known as a 'contingency fee' because the payment is contingent upon success. If the client loses the case, the solicitor does not receive a fee.

For some time there has been uncertainty as to whether it is open to a defendant to enter into a DBA. Logic would suggest that given the link between the fee and damages recovered, such agreements are only available to claimants, or can perhaps extend to defendants with a substantial counterclaim. This appears to have been settled by *Candey Ltd v Tonstate Group Ltd* [2022] EWCA Civ 936 in which it was held that a non-counterclaiming defendant could not enter into a DBA. However, at the date of writing, it is thought that the decision may be appealed.

Under a DBA, if the client wins the case the solicitor receives the agreed percentage of the damages recovered. The amount paid by the client will be net of any costs payable by the opponent. So, any costs to be paid by the opponent will be set off against the contingency fee and the client will only have to pay the balance. If the client loses the case, the effect mirrors that of a CFA, in that the client will not be responsible for their own solicitor's fees, but may still be liable for the disbursements as well as, usually, having to pay the opponent's costs. Therefore, as with a CFA, it may also be appropriate to combine a DBA with ATE insurance cover (see **7.7.2.1** and **7.7.3.2**).

⊗ *Example*

A firm of solicitors is instructed by Alpha Ltd in a contract dispute. The firm enters into a DBA with Alpha Ltd which is set at 20%. At trial, Alpha Ltd wins their claim and recover damages of £100,000 from the defendant, together with £15,000 towards Alpha Ltd's costs.

Under the DBA, Alpha Ltd will owe the firm £20,000 by way of a contingency fee to cover their legal fees. However, £15,000 will be covered by their opponent, leaving a shortfall of £5000 for which the client remains responsible. This will be deducted from the damages so that Alpha Ltd will actually receive £95,000 in total.

A DBA is subject to a cap on the level of the solicitor's fee. The DBA must not provide for a payment above an amount which, including VAT, is equal to 50% of the sums ultimately recovered by the client. The cap is inclusive of counsel's fees, but not other disbursements for which the client will remain liable. The cap does not apply to appeal proceedings.

A lower cap is set in personal injury cases, namely 25% of general damages received for pain, suffering, and loss of amenity and damages for pecuniary loss (other than future pecuniary loss). The cap for employment cases is 35%. Again the cap does not apply to appeals.

To be enforceable a DBA must meet the requirements of s 58AA(4) Courts and Legal Services Act 1990 and the Damages-Based Agreements Regulations 2013 (SI 2013/609). In essence this means that the agreement must be in writing and specify the proceedings to which the agreement relates, the circumstances in which the fee is payable and the reason for setting the fee at the level agreed. If the DBA is adjudged unenforceable, the client will not have to pay the solicitor anything.

There is some uncertainty as to the precise requirements of the legislation which has led to a reluctance amongst some solicitors to enter into DBAs rather than risk the DBA being adjudged unenforceable and losing out on their fees. Some clarification was provided in the following case:

Zuberi v Lexlaw Ltd [2021] EWCA Civ 16

In this case the client was bringing a claim against two banks for the mis-selling of financial products. The firm agreed to act for the client under a DBA which provided that the firm would be paid 10% of the damages received. The DBA also provided that in the event of the client terminating the agreement before the conclusion of the case, the client would pay for the work done to date.

The firm worked on the case for some considerable time. Then over a short period of time, in rapid succession, the banks indicated that they would be making an improved offer of settlement, the client terminated the retainer with the firm and the case was settled on the basis that the client would receive damages of £1 million.

The firm then sought their fee of £125,000, but the client refused to pay anything. The client argued that the clause requiring 'normal' payment in the event of early termination of the agreement breached s 58AA Courts and Legal Services Act 1990 and that, as a consequence, the DBA was void and unenforceable.

The Court of Appeal held that s 58AA (and the regulations made under it) did not prevent a firm being paid in the event of early termination of the agreement by the client. The case is also authority for the use of so-called 'hybrid-DBAs' whereby a firm may receive concurrent funding via a DBA and some other form of retainer (eg discounted hourly charging rates in the event that the client loses the case).

As a means of funding DBAs have not proved to be particularly popular. From the solicitor's perspective DBAs are often not commercially attractive simply because the level of damages awarded in civil litigation means that often the fees received do not even cover basic costs. In addition, entering into a DBA represents a considerable risk. The nature of a DBA is such that it is only a viable option where the solicitor is confident not only that the client will succeed, but also that the opponent will pay both the damages and costs from which the solicitor's fees will be taken.

From the client's perspective a DBA may provide access to justice at relatively little risk. However, the client may still feel aggrieved when the solicitor 'takes' a significant slice of the damages in fees having apparently done little work (for example, if the case is settled early in the proceedings). In some cases this may result in the client seeking to avoid paying the full amount by raising objections with the court based on proportionality.

7.7.2.3 Comparison of CFAs and DBAs

- The enhanced rate is calculated by reference to an uplift in the solicitor's usual hourly charging rate in CFAs, but is linked to the damages received in DBAs.

- The success fee is limited to 100% of the usual hourly rate in CFAs; but the contingency fee cannot exceed 50% of the damages in DBAs.

- In both arrangements, the client is not required to pay their solicitor's fee if the case does not succeed, or pays a lesser amount depending upon the agreement.

- Neither CFAs nor DBAs cover the client's own disbursements, or the opponent's costs, which must be dealt with separately.

- Both must be in writing.

- The availability and terms of these funding arrangements will reflect the infinite variety of cases and the inherent difficulties of predicting the outcome of litigation.

7.7.3   Legal expenses insurance

7.7.3.1   Before-the-event insurance (BTE)

A client may have an insurance policy which will cover payment of their solicitor's fees (often called before-the-event insurance). It is possible to obtain a policy specifically for the purpose of covering legal expenses. However, such insurance is commonly purchased as part of household or motor insurance policies. Therefore, at the outset of the matter, a solicitor should establish whether the client already has legal expenses insurance in place. According to Lord Phillips MR (delivering the judgment of the Court) in *Sarwar v Alam* [2001] EWCA Civ 1401:

> In our judgment, proper modern practice dictates that a solicitor should normally invite a client to bring to the first interview any relevant motor insurance policy, any household insurance policy and any stand-alone before-the-event insurance policy belonging to the client and/or any spouse or partner living in the same household as the client.

An insurance policy is unlikely to cover legal expenses in every type of case, and so the precise terms of the individual policy must be examined. Typically, motor insurance will cover aspects of the vehicle ownership and household insurance will cover expenses involved with one or more of the following: ownership of the property, employment, personal injury, sale of goods and supply of services. Even where the subject matter is covered, the policy may exclude or limit certain costs.

As with any insurance, in order to take advantage of the terms of the policy the insurer must first accept the claim. The insurer may not accept the claim if, for example, the case does not have a good prospect of success (generally more than 50%) or the case concerns issues that arose before the policy was taken out.

An issue which can arise with legal expense insurance is that the insurer will usually wish the case to be conducted by a firm on its own panel of solicitors. However, at least from the point of the start of proceedings the client is entitled to instruct a solicitor of their own choosing.

In a litigation matter the solicitor should also establish whether any insurance policy covers the client's liability for another party's costs. If not, it may be possible for the client to purchase after-the-event insurance to cover such liability.

7.7.3.2   After-the-event insurance (ATE)

ATE covers the legal expenses incurred in making or defending a case. It is available for most types of civil litigation with the exception of family law. As the name suggests the insurance is taken out after the dispute has arisen.

The cover provided by the policy will be specific to the case and the client's needs. Whilst it is possible to obtain ATE to cover the client's own legal fees, ATE usually covers liability for disbursements and the opponent's costs. ATE is often coupled with a CFA (see **7.7.2.1**) which does not protect the client from liability for the opponent's costs in the event of losing the case.

The client will have to find an insurer willing to take on the risk. ATE will only be offered where the insurer is confident in the success of the case (for most insurers this means a 60% chance of success).

Given the fact that, by definition, a dispute has already arisen ATE may be expensive to obtain. The premium payable will depend on the strength of the client's case and the level of cover required. It may be possible to arrange a 'staged' premium, whereby additional instalments are paid if the case continues beyond certain defined stages. The client will bear the cost of taking out ATE themselves as the premium is not recoverable from the other side by way of costs.

Figure 7.1 Comparison flowchart

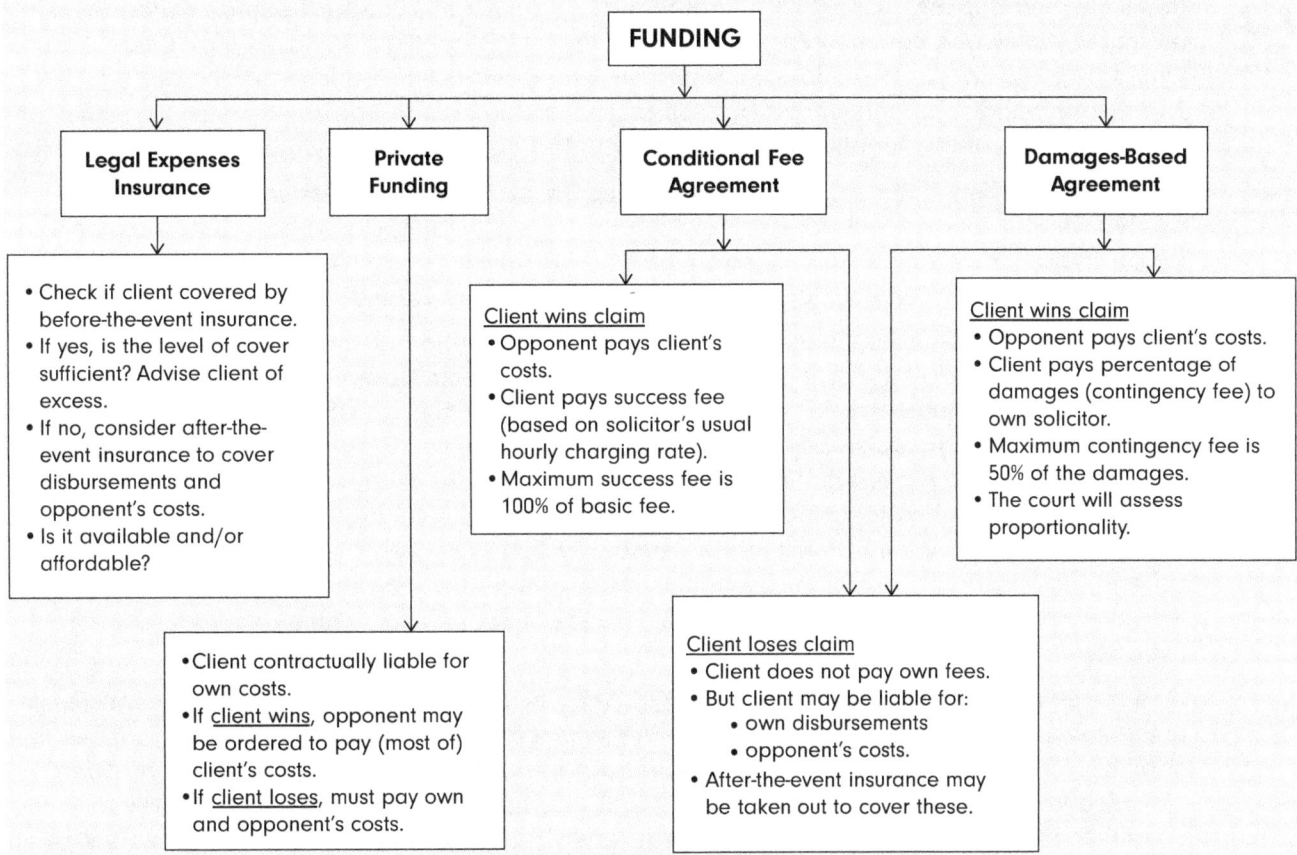

```
                              ┌──────────────┐
                              │   FUNDING    │
                              └──────────────┘
```

| Legal Expenses Insurance | Private Funding | Conditional Fee Agreement | Damages-Based Agreement |

Legal Expenses Insurance

- Check if client covered by before-the-event insurance.
- If yes, is the level of cover sufficient? Advise client of excess.
- If no, consider after-the-event insurance to cover disbursements and opponent's costs.
- Is it available and/or affordable?

Private Funding

- Client contractually liable for own costs.
- If <u>client wins</u>, opponent may be ordered to pay (most of) client's costs.
- If <u>client loses</u>, must pay own and opponent's costs.

Conditional Fee Agreement

<u>Client wins claim</u>
- Opponent pays client's costs.
- Client pays success fee (based on solicitor's usual hourly charging rate).
- Maximum success fee is 100% of basic fee.

<u>Client loses claim</u>
- Client does not pay own fees.
- But client may be liable for:
  - own disbursements
  - opponent's costs.
- After-the-event insurance may be taken out to cover these.

Damages-Based Agreement

<u>Client wins claim</u>
- Opponent pays client's costs.
- Client pays percentage of damages (contingency fee) to own solicitor.
- Maximum contingency fee is 50% of the damages.
- The court will assess proportionality.

A solicitor who recommends or arranges ATE for a client will be carrying out insurance distribution activities. The solicitor must take account of the restrictions imposed by the Financial Services and Markets Act 2000 (see **Chapter 4**).

7.7.4 Third party funding

As the name suggests third party funding (also known as 'litigation funding' or 'litigation finance') describes the situation where someone, with no other connection to the case, agrees to fund the costs of litigation. For some clients the source of funding may be a trade union or professional organisation which in certain circumstances will agree to be responsible for payment of the legal costs of their members. However, for most clients third party funding will involve a specialist litigation funding company which will agree to fund the costs of litigation in return for a fee payable from money received by the litigant at the end of the case.

Historically, the commercial funding of litigation was outlawed on public policy grounds, essentially on the basis that a third party would seek to manipulate the litigation, inflate damages and thereby taint the judicial process. However, in recent years, commercial funding has become accepted such that a third party funding agreement will be valid in the absence of some kind of impropriety or wrongdoing. For example, in the case which is said to have paved the way for the introduction of third party funding, *Arkin v Borchard Lines Ltd* [2005] EWCA Civ 655, the court affirmed 'the commercial funder who is financing part of the costs of the litigation in a manner which facilitates access to justice and which is not otherwise objectionable'.

Third party funding is primarily used by commercial claimants. It is not unknown for individual claimants, but as a matter of policy commercial funders do not fund personal injury and consumer cases. Commercial funders take their fee from the money recovered at the end of the case and so third party funding is not usually available to defendants. However, some commercial funders are willing to provide funding for defendants who have a substantial counterclaim.

A commercial funder will only take on a case where there is a good chance of success. Most funders interpret this as meaning that the chance of success must be at least 60%. The size of the likely award is also important in that it must be sufficient to cover the funder's fee. As a matter of policy and commercial pragmatism funders do not take on cases where the litigant would be left with less than 50% of the amount recovered after deduction of the funder's fee. The funder will also be influenced by such factors as the strength or any counterclaim, the likely timescale of the litigation and the ability of the opponent to pay.

Third party funding is aimed at covering the client's own costs and disbursements. However, exactly what is covered will depend on the terms of the funding agreement. It is common, for example, for the funder to only cover part of the solicitor's fees with the remainder being covered by the client or via a CFA (see **7.7.2.1**) or DBA (see **7.7.2.2**).

If the case is successful the funder will receive their fee from the amount recovered by the client. How the fee is calculated depends on the terms of the funding agreement. Various methods of calculation are employed, for example, the fee may be a multiple of the amount spent on legal fees. In *R (on the application of PACAAR Inc) v Competition Appeal Tribunal* [2023] UKSC 28, the Supreme Court ruled that agreements which provide for the funder's fee to be calculated as a percentage of the amount recovered are DBAs and, as such, are unenforceable unless they comply with the regulations governing DBAs (see **7.7.2.2**). However, the Civil Justice Council is currently undertaking a review to determine, inter alia, whether legislation should be introduced to return the position to that which existed before the Supreme Court ruling (the final report is expected to be produced in summer 2025).

One issue which can arise in relation to third party funding is liability for the opponent's costs in the event that the client loses the case. The *Arkin* case (above) placed a limit or cap on the liability of the commercial funder. However, in *Chapelgate Credit Opportunity Master Fund Ltd v Money and others* [2020] EWCA Civ 246 it was held that costs are in the discretion of the court with the result that the funder was ordered to pay all the opponent's costs from the date of the funding agreement. Similarly, in Laser Trust v CFL Finance Ltd [2021] EWHC 1404 (Ch), a third party costs order (not subject to a cap) was justified given the level of control that the funder had over the proceedings. Commercial funders will factor in this potential liability to their fees and/or their willingness to offer funding in the first place.

Any solicitor acting for a client under third party funding must have regard to their professional conduct responsibilities. Minimising the influence which the funder has over the conduct of the case will reduce the risk of a conflict of interest arising (see **Ethics and Professional Conduct**). Similarly the solicitor must be wary of breaching client confidentiality (see **Ethics and Professional Conduct**) when asked to provide the funder with information and/or documentation relating to the case.

Summary

The main funding options are:

- Private funding – the client pays for the work done based on the solicitor's hourly charging rate.
- Fixed fees – the client pays a set amount for work done.
- Conditional fee arrangements – if client wins the solicitor receives an enhanced fee calculated as a percentage of the solicitor's usual charging rate. If the client loses the solicitor receives a lower fee or no fee.
- Damages-based agreement – if the client wins the solicitor receives a percentage of the damages received. If the client loses the solicitor receives no fee.
- Before-the-event insurance – the solicitor's fees are covered by an existing policy (eg a household insurance policy).

- After-the-event insurance – a policy usually taken out to cover the client's own disbursements and liability for the opponent's costs in the event of the client losing.
- Third party funding – a third party (usually a commercial funder) agrees to fund the litigation.

Sample questions

Question 1

A solicitor agrees to act for a client on a 'no win, no fee' conditional fee agreement with a success fee of 25%.

Which of the following describes the costs position?

A   If the client wins, the solicitor's fee will be calculated at 25% of the damages received.

B   If the client wins, the opponent will pay the success fee.

C   If the client wins, the client will pay nothing in respect of their own costs.

D   If the client loses, the client will have to pay disbursements.

E   If the client loses, the solicitor's fee will be calculated at their usual charging rate.

Answer

Option D is correct. This is a 'no win, no fee' CFA, so if the client loses they will not have to pay anything in fees, but will still be liable for disbursements (and the opponent's costs). In a CFA the success fee is calculated as a percentage of the usual charging rate, not a percentage of the damages received. If the client wins they will have to pay the success fee as it cannot be recovered from the opponent.

Question 2

A junior solicitor is approached by a wealthy individual in relation to a personal injury claim. The solicitor's assessment of the case is that there is a good chance of obtaining substantial damages. The solicitor tells the prospective client that the firm has a strict policy of not acting on the basis of contingency fees. Nevertheless, the prospective client requests that the case be dealt with under a damages-based agreement (DBA).

Which of the following best explains whether the solicitor should agree or refuse to act under a DBA?

A   Refuse, because that is the firm's policy.

B   Refuse, because the client can afford to pay privately for the solicitor's costs.

C   Agree, because the client has the right to decide how their legal costs are funded.

D   Agree, because to do so is in the client's best interests.

E   Agree, because the risk to the firm is low.

Answer

Option A is correct. It is for the client to decide how their costs are funded, but that does not impose an obligation on the part of a firm to act for a client on a particular basis. Therefore a firm may refuse to act under a DBA as a matter of policy. A junior solicitor should adhere to the firm's policy even if the risk to the firm in an individual case is low. If it is in the client's best interests to have a DBA the client should be referred to another firm.

Question 3

A solicitor agrees to carry out a conveyancing transaction for a client at a fixed fee of £500 plus VAT and disbursements. A month into the transaction, it becomes clear that the solicitor will have to undertake much more work than was originally envisaged.

Which of the following best describes what the solicitor can do?

A   Tell the client that the solicitor can no longer act for the client.

B   Start charging the client on the basis of the solicitor's hourly charging rate.

C   Ask the client to agree to an increase in the solicitor's fees.

D   Write to the client providing the best possible information on the revised overall costs.

E   Carry out no further work on the transaction pending the client agreeing to an increase in fees.

Answer

Option C is correct. A fixed fee cannot be changed at a later date if it transpires that the case is more expensive than originally thought (save with the client's agreement). Although it is not a step to be undertaken lightly, all that the solicitor can do is to ask the client to agree to an increase. If the client refuses, the solicitor must complete the work for the fee agreed.

8 Legal Aid

SQE1 syllabus

This chapter will enable you to achieve the SQE1 Assessment Specification in relation to Functioning Legal Knowledge concerned with Legal Services:

- Funding options for legal services.
- Eligibility for civil legal aid.
- Eligibility for criminal legal aid.

Note that for SQE1, candidates are not usually required to recall specific case names or cite statutory or regulatory authorities. Cases are provided for illustrative purposes only.

Learning outcomes

By the end of this chapter you will be able to apply relevant core legal principles and rules appropriately and effectively, at the level of a competent newly qualified solicitor in practice, to realistic client-based and ethical problems and situations in the following areas:

- Civil and criminal legal aid.
- The scope of legal aid.
- Individual client eligibility.
- Means tests.
- Merits tests.
- The statutory charge.

8.1 Introduction

Legal aid is the means by which those who are eligible can have some or all of their legal fees paid from public funds (legal aid is sometimes referred to as 'public funding'). Legal aid in both civil and criminal cases is primarily governed by the Legal Aid, Sentencing and Punishment of Offenders Act 2012, although much of the detail appears in a range of statutory instruments. The legal aid scheme is administered by the Legal Aid Agency, an executive agency of the Ministry of Justice.

This chapter looks at:

- the solicitor and the Legal Aid Agency
- civil legal aid
- criminal legal aid

8.2 The solicitor and the Legal Aid Agency

To carry out legal aid work, a firm of solicitors must have a contract with the Legal Aid Agency which covers the type of work relevant to the client's case, eg criminal defence work, care proceedings, immigration and so on. Firms which have been awarded a contract are subject to an annual audit by the Legal Aid Agency to ensure that their files are being run properly and that the firm's case management systems are working correctly.

Even if a firm has a relevant contract with the Legal Aid Agency, this does not oblige the firm to accept instructions from the client and/or act for the client under the legal aid scheme (save under the duty solicitor scheme – see **8.4.2**). Just as with any other client, the firm is still entitled to take a view of the case overall and, if it is considered to be unremunerative, decline to act. If instructions are declined, it may be appropriate to advise the client to seek legal advice elsewhere.

If a solicitor does not undertake legal aid work themselves, but is of the view that the client may be entitled to legal aid, the solicitor should inform the client accordingly at the outset of the case and, if necessary, tell the client to seek other advice.

David Truex, Solicitor (a firm) v Kitchin [2007] EWCA Civ 618

In this case the Court of Appeal held that a solicitor must from the outset of a case consider whether a client might be eligible for legal aid. The Court observed that if the financial position of the client had been considered properly, and considered in the context of whether they might be eligible for legal aid, the result would have been advice to go to a different firm offering legal aid at a very early stage. The solicitor had failed to give this advice and, as a result, the firm was denied its fees.

Acting for a client who is in receipt of legal aid places additional duties on the solicitor. For example, the solicitor must inform the court and the other parties that the client has the benefit of legal aid. Whilst the solicitor will still owe the usual professional conduct duties to the client, the solicitor will also have separate duties to the Legal Aid Agency. For example, the solicitor must inform the Legal Aid Agency if the client acts unreasonably (eg refuses a reasonable offer of settlement) or has given inaccurate or misleading information to the Legal Aid Agency. This duty to the Legal Aid Agency overrides the solicitor's duty of confidentiality to the client (see **Ethics and Professional Conduct**).

At the end of the case the solicitor will claim their costs from the Legal Aid Agency. There are set levels of remuneration for legal aid work which are usually lower than the amount which a solicitor would charge a privately paying client in an equivalent case.

8.3   Civil legal aid

In the past those of modest means who could demonstrate that their case had merit were entitled to have their legal fees paid through the legal aid scheme. In recent years however, civil legal aid has been severely curtailed and is now only available in limited circumstances.

The civil legal aid scheme is hugely detailed and complex. This manual can only provide a broad and general overview of the basic scheme. It should be noted that certain types of cases (such as immigration cases and family cases) fall under subject-specific rules and regulations which are beyond the scope of this manual.

8.3.1   Forms of civil services

The legislation refers to solicitors providing 'forms of civil services', in other words types of legal aid work. Civil legal aid falls into two categories: controlled work and licensed work. Broadly, with controlled work it is for the solicitor to determine the client's eligibility, whereas licensed work is authorised by the Legal Aid Agency on a case by case basis.

Within these two categories there are three forms of civil services available (there are more forms of civil services available in family cases). The application of each form is based broadly on how litigious the case becomes. Between them these forms of civil services can cover a range of legal work, from basic advice to advocacy before the court.

8.3.1.1   Legal Help

This covers the solicitor giving basic advice and limited steps following on from that advice. This might involve drafting a letter or obtaining information from a third party. It does not extend to issuing court proceedings. Legal Help is controlled work.

8.3.1.2   Help at Court

This type of funding covers advice and assistance, including advocacy. The work which the solicitor carries out must be in relation to a particular hearing rather than representation in the case generally. A typical case in which Help at Court would be used is where a client is subject to possession proceedings to which there is no defence, but the client needs help in putting arguments to the court with the aim of postponing or delaying eviction. Help at Court is controlled work.

8.3.1.3   Legal Representation

Legal Representation is available to a client who is a party to proceedings or who is contemplating starting proceedings. It can cover the conduct of the client's case, if necessary, up to and including representation before the court.

Legal Representation is licensed work. This means that in most cases an application must be made to the Legal Aid Agency. If the application is successful the Legal Aid Agency will issue a legal aid certificate.

Legal Representation can be granted on an investigative or full basis. Investigative representation covers the solicitor's work in assessing the strength of the case. Full representation covers the issuing and conduct of the proceedings, including advocacy at the final hearing. In practice the Legal Aid Agency will usually place limitations on the legal aid certificate which restricts the scope of the representation which can be given and/or sets a maximum amount that it will pay for legal fees. If the case requires more work, the solicitor must apply for an amendment to the certificate and/or an increase of the costs limitation.

Legal Representation can be obtained on an emergency basis where the client is in urgent need of legal advice and assistance. This might be appropriate, for example, if the client is facing imminent homelessness or under threat of domestic violence.

8.3.2 The scope of legal aid

For legal aid to even arise as a possible funding option the case must be of a type which falls within the overall scope of the civil legal aid scheme. Legal aid is only available for a case if it is of a type specified under Sch 1, Pt 1 Legal Aid, Sentencing and Punishment of Offenders Act 2012.

Legal aid is not available for large areas of legal work. For example, with limited exceptions, negligence claims for personal injury, divorce and family disputes about children are excluded. Legal aid is not available for matters arising out of the carrying on of a business, including claims brought or defended by sole traders. In addition legal aid will not usually be available for cases that could be financed by a Conditional Fee Arrangement (see **7.7.2**).

Cases where legal aid remains available include those where the client faces homelessness, family cases where the client is the victim of domestic abuse, cases in which the client has been subject to discrimination, immigration cases and care proceedings.

Even if a case falls outside the scope of legal aid, it may still be possible to obtain funding if the circumstances are 'exceptional'. Legal aid will be granted in any case where the Legal Aid Agency is satisfied that refusal would be a breach of the client's human rights. That is a high threshold and so the number of successful applications for exceptional case funding remains relatively small. Nevertheless it remains an option where the interests of justice require.

Where a case falls within the scope of legal aid or is suitable for exceptional case funding it is still necessary to demonstrate that the client is eligible based on the merits of the case and the client's financial circumstances.

8.3.3 Merits test

The legislation sets out a number of merits tests to be applied depending on the form of civil services required and the nature of the case. Although the details vary, the tests all involve an assessment of the client's prospects of success and the application of a cost–benefit criteria.

Legal Help and Help at Court are subject to the 'sufficient benefit test'. Legal aid will only be available if there is a sufficient benefit to the client, having regard to the circumstances of the case, including the client's personal circumstances, to justify the work being carried out.

Legal Representation is dependant of the client's prospects of success. Broadly, Legal Representation will not be granted if those prospects are assessed at less than 50%. In addition the client must satisfy a general merits test or a specific merits test depending on the type of case. For example, if the case involves a monetary claim the merits test will involve a balancing of the damages that are likely to be received against the likely costs involved in the case. In a non-monetary case the test is whether the benefits to be gained justify the likely cost such that a reasonable privately paying client would be prepared to proceed (the 'reasonable privately paying client test').

Legal representation will also be refused if the Legal Aid Agency takes the view that other funding is available to the client (for example legal expense insurance) or if the case is suitable for a Conditional Fee Arrangement (see **7.7.2**).

8.3.4 Means test

A client will only qualify for legal aid if their capital and income (combined with the resources of any partner) does not exceed certain limits. The client is required to produce full details of their financial circumstances in order to enable the means test to be carried out.

The capital limit for civil legal aid is £8,000 (£3,000 for immigration cases). If the client has capital of more than £8,000, they do not qualify for legal aid and there is no need to consider the client's income position.

A client in receipt of one of a number of welfare benefits (primarily universal credit, but also ongoing entitlement to income support, income-based job seeker's allowance, income-related employment and support allowance, guarantee credit element of pension credit) automatically qualifies for legal aid on the basis of income, but their capital must still be assessed.

For other clients the income test first considers the client's gross income. If the client's gross monthly income exceeds £2,657 the client does not qualify for legal aid (the figure is slightly higher if the client has five or more children). If the client's gross monthly income is £2,567 or less the assessment goes on to make certain deductions (to reflect the client's family circumstances and their basic living expenses) to arrive at a figure for the client's disposable income. The client will only qualify for legal aid if their monthly disposable income is less than £733.

Even where the client's capital and income is below these limits, the means assessment may reveal that the client can afford to pay something towards their legal costs. For licensed work (for example, legal representation) if the client's monthly disposable income is above £315 or their capital above £3,000 legal aid will be offered to the client on the basis that they make a contribution towards their legal fees. If the contribution is from income it will take the form of monthly payments.

⭐ Example

Nilu applies for legal aid in the form of Legal Representation. Nilu has capital of £4,000 and her gross income is £1,500 (Nilu's monthly disposable income is £300).

Nilu's capital is less than £8,000. Nilu's gross income is below the £2,567 monthly limit and her disposable income is below the £733 limit. Therefore, provided that she satisfies the merits test, Nilu is eligible for legal aid on the basis of both capital and income. However, as Nilu's capital exceeds £3,000 legal aid will be offered to her on the basis that she makes a capital contribution to her legal fees.

8.3.5 The statutory charge

Legal aid does not necessarily amount to free legal representation for the client. In broad terms, if the client benefits financially from the case, any money or property the client receives can be used in repayment of the solicitor's fees. This is the so-called statutory charge.

For the statutory charge to arise the client must have been wholly or partly successful in the proceedings, or obtained an out-of-court settlement which resulted in the client gaining or keeping money or property. Usually (but not invariably) the client must have been in receipt of Legal Representation.

In all cases the Legal Aid Agency will attempt to recoup the money it has paid on the client's behalf. In order to do so, it will first claim any money paid pursuant to a costs order made in the client's favour. Secondly, if a shortfall remains, the Legal Aid Agency will retain any contribution paid by the client under the terms of the offer of legal aid. Thirdly, if there is still a deficit any money recovered or preserved in the proceedings will be applied to make up the shortfall.

To facilitate collection of the statutory charge, the solicitor is required to pass any money payable to the client under a court order or out-of-court settlement to the Legal Aid Agency. Usually the statutory charge is payable immediately. However, if the property recovered is the client's home the Legal Aid Agency may agree to postpone enforcement of the statutory charge. If enforcement is postponed the statutory charge will be protected by registration against title to the property (and simple interest applied) so that the fees will be recouped when the property is eventually sold.

Given the obvious financial implications of the statutory charge it is vital that the client fully understands how it operates and is reminded of it throughout the case. The client should also be advised periodically as to the costs incurred to date.

8.4 Criminal legal aid

Public funding is also available for the cost of a defendant's legal representation in criminal cases before both the magistrates' court and the crown court. Criminal legal aid is more widely available than civil legal aid. Nevertheless there are strict eligibility criteria set out in a number of statutory instruments.

8.4.1 Advice at the police station

Anyone attending at the police station (whether under arrest, or attending voluntarily) is entitled to free legal advice, irrespective of their means. The solicitor will claim for the work done under the Police Station Advice and Assistance Scheme. The solicitor will receive a single fixed fee regardless of the nature of the case or the time actually spent (although there is special provision for very serious or unusually time-consuming cases).

Most criminal defence solicitors take part in the duty scheme for a particular police station. The solicitor's name is placed on a rota, and when 'on duty' they will be called out to attend the police station to advise anyone who has been arrested and does not have their own solicitor.

8.4.2 The duty solicitor scheme

Some solicitors are members of the duty solicitor scheme. A duty solicitor will be on a rota to attend a magistrates' court on given days. The duty solicitor is available to advise any defendant who does not have their own solicitor but who requires legal advice and/ or representation. The duty solicitor will claim their costs in attending court from under the Advocacy Assistance (Court Duty Solicitor) Scheme.

The scheme operates in a similar way to that in respect of police stations.

8.4.3 Application for legal aid

A client who has been charged with a criminal offence and who wishes to seek public funding for their legal fees in respect of the resultant proceedings must make an application for criminal legal aid. Legal aid will only be granted if the client is able to demonstrate that both the merits of the case and their own financial means are such as to justify public funding. The client will therefore have to satisfy two tests.

8.4.3.1 The interests of justice test

This test assesses the merits of the case. The client must demonstrate that it is in the interests of justice for them to receive public funding to cover the cost of their legal representation.

A number of factors are taken into account in deciding whether a client can satisfy the interests of justice test (s 17 Legal Aid, Sentencing and Punishment of Offenders Act 2012):

(a) whether the individual would, if any matter arising in the proceedings is decided against them, be likely to lose their liberty or livelihood or suffer serious damage to their reputation;

(b) whether the determination of any matter arising in the proceedings may involve consideration of a substantial question of law;

(c) whether the individual may be unable to understand the proceedings or to state their own case;

(d) whether the proceedings may involve the tracing, interviewing or expert cross-examination of witnesses on behalf of the individual; and

(e) whether it is in the interests of another person that the individual be represented (note that the other 'person' referred to here will most commonly be a prosecution witness in a sensitive case where it would not be appropriate for the defendant to cross-examine them in person).

Additionally, there is a catch-all provision under which it is open to the client to demonstrate that there is 'some other reason' making it in the interests of justice for them to receive legal aid.

Each of these factors must be considered and weighed. One or more may be applicable to a varying extent depending on the particular facts of the client's case. Broadly, the more serious the consequences for the client or the more complex the proceedings, the more likely it is that the client will be able to satisfy the test.

The interests of justice test is considered in more detail in **Criminal Practice**.

8.4.3.2   Means test

Clients who are under 18 or who receive one of a number of welfare benefits (primarily universal credit, but also ongoing entitlement to income support, income-based jobseeker's allowance, guaranteed state pension credit, income-based employment and support allowance) are automatically entitled to criminal legal aid without needing to satisfy the means test.

All other clients will need to submit full details of their financial circumstances. Initially a rudimentary assessment will be carried out by taking the client's gross annual income and dividing it by a set figure according to whether the client has a partner and/or children. This produces a figure for the client's 'adjusted income'. For magistrates' court cases the level of adjusted income will either put the client at one end of the spectrum by determining that the client is eligible or not, or put the client into the middle ground which necessitates a full means test being carried out. For crown court trials, those at the higher end of the spectrum will also be subject to a full means test.

Adjusted income	Magistrates' court	Crown court trial
£12,475 or less	Eligible	Eligible
more than £12,475 – less than £22,325	Full means test	Full means test
£22,325 and above	Not eligible	Full means test

The full means test is more sophisticated as it takes account of the client's family circumstances and involves the deduction of some essential expenses from the client's income, such as mortgage repayments or rent, to produce a figure for the client's disposable income. For cases before the magistrates' court the purpose of the means test is to determine whether the client is eligible for legal aid or not: to be entitled to legal aid the client must have an annual disposable income of £3,398 or less. For crown court trials, if a client has a disposable income of more than £3,398 and less than £37,500, the means test may determine that the client can afford to make some contribution towards their legal fees, whether from income or capital, and legal aid will be offered to the client on that basis.

8.4.3.3   Representation order

The result of a successful application for criminal legal aid is that a representation order will be issued and sent to the solicitor. This is in effect confirmation that the solicitor may start incurring legal costs on the client's behalf which will be covered under the legal aid scheme. Depending on the terms of the representation order it will cover the costs of conducting the case for the client. If appropriate, the terms of the representation order can be extended, for example to cover the costs of an appeal.

Summary

- The legal aid scheme enables those who qualify to have their legal fees paid from public funds.

- Only firms with a relevant contract with the Legal Aid Agency can carry out legal aid work.

- The solicitor has an ongoing relationship with the Legal Aid Agency throughout the client's case and owes certain duties to the Legal Aid Agency.

- The main forms of civil services are Legal Help, Help at Court and Legal Representation.

- Civil legal aid is only available for a limited range of cases.

- To qualify for civil legal aid the client must satisfy tests as to their own means and the merits of the case.

- The statutory charge operates so that the client may have to repay their legal fees from money or property received or preserved in the proceedings.

- Criminal legal aid is available for advice at the police station, under the duty solicitor scheme and by application for a representation order.

- To qualify for a representation order the client must satisfy the interests of justice test and the means test.

Sample questions

Question 1

A solicitor is instructed by a client in a claim for damages. The client is in receipt of universal credit and has capital of £1,000. The solicitor is confident that the case has a good chance of success and satisfies the merits test. The client submits an application for legal aid in the form of Legal Representation.

Which of the following describes the costs position if the application is successful?

A   The client will be asked to make a monthly contribution towards their legal fees.

B   The client is entitled to free legal representation.

C   The client may have to repay some of their legal fees.

D   The solicitor can choose to charge for the work done at any hourly rate.

E   The solicitor can insist that the client pay money on account of costs.

Answer

Option C is correct. If the client is awarded damages in the case, the effect of the statutory charge is that the client may have to repay some of their legal fees. Therefore the representation is not free (option B therefore is wrong). The client's means are not such as would require them to make a contribution towards their legal fees (option A is wrong). The solicitor will be remunerated at set levels (option D is wrong). Finally, option E is wrong as the solicitor must look to the Legal Aid Agency for payment of their fees and so the solicitor cannot ask the client to pay money on account.

Question 2

A solicitor is instructed by a client who is the defendant in possession proceedings. If the claimant succeeds in the case the client will be evicted and become homeless. However, the solicitor is confident that the client has a good defence and would win the case. The client has no capital and is in receipt of universal credit.

Is the client likely to be eligible for legal aid in respect of the proceedings?

A   No, because civil legal aid is only available to claimants.

B   No, because the case falls outside the scope of legal aid.

C   No, because a reasonable privately paying client would not be prepared to proceed with the case.

D   Yes, because a client in receipt of universal credit automatically qualifies for legal aid.

E   Yes, because the client satisfies both the means and the merits test.

Answer

Option E is correct. Legal aid is available to both claimants and defendants; accordingly, option A is wrong. A case in which the client is faced with homelessness is within the scope of legal aid; option B is wrong. The 'reasonable privately paying client' test would be satisfied given the threat of homelessness and the client has a good chance of success; option C therefore is wrong. Option D is wrong, as a client in receipt of universal credit does not automatically qualify for legal aid – they must still satisfy the merits test and the capital element of the means test. On these facts the client satisfies both the merits test (as above) and means tests (the client is in receipt of universal credit and has capital of less than £8,000).

Question 3

A solicitor is instructed by a client who is the defendant in criminal proceedings. The client is charged with stealing from their employer. The case will be dealt with by way of a crown court trial. The client has no capital and is not in receipt of any welfare benefits.

Which of the following best describes the position with regard to the client's eligibility for legal aid in respect of the trial?

A   Legal aid will not be granted if the risk of the client receiving a custodial sentence is low.

B   Legal aid will only be granted if a reasonable privately paying client would proceed with the case.

C   Legal aid will be granted if the client's annual adjusted income is £10,000.

D   Legal aid will be granted because the client has no capital.

E   Legal aid is unlikely to be granted unless a conviction for stealing from an employer would result in serious damage to the client's reputation.

Answer

Option C is correct. To be eligible for criminal legal aid the client must satisfy both the interests of justice test and the means test. In a crown court trial the interests of justice test is automatically satisfied, so option E is wrong. The client has no capital, but their income is relevant for the means test (option D is wrong). An adjusted income figure below the limit of £12,475 satisfies the means test and therefore legal aid will be granted. The reasonable privately paying client test is relevant for civil legal aid (option B is therefore wrong).

Index